P9-ELR-685

56 ARCHEOLOGY

57 ARCTIC & ANTARCTIC

58 BUILDING

59 PIRATE

60 NORTH AMERICAN INDIAN

AFRICA

OCEAN

63 BATTLE

64 GORILLA, MONKEY & APE

65 MEDIEVAL LIFE

66 FARM

67 SPY

RELIGION

EAGLE & BIRDS OF PREY

70 WITCHES & MAGIC-MAKERS

71 SPACE EXPLORATION

72 SHIPWRECK

73 CRIME & DETECTION

74 RUSSIA

75 LIGHT

76 ENERGY

77 ELECTRICITY

78 FORCE & MOTION

79 CHEMISTRY

80 MATTER

81 TIME & SPACE

82 ASTRONOMY

83 EARTH

84 LIFE

85 EVOLUTION

86 ECOLOGY

87 HUMAN BODY

88 MEDICINE

89 TECHNOLOGY

90 ELECTRONICS

91 RENAISSANCE

92 IMPRESSIONISM

93 GOYA

94 MANET

95 MONET

96 VAN GOGH

97 WATERCOLOR

98 PERSPECTIVE

99 DANCE

100 FUTURE

101 MYTHOLOGY

102 LEONARDO & HIS TIMES

103 OLYMPICS

104 MEDIA & COMMUNICATION

105 TITANIC

106 FOOTBALL

107 HURRICANE & TORNADO

108 SOCCER

109 PRESIDENTS

110 BASEBALL

DORLING KINDERSLEY 📖 EYEWITNESS BOOKS

SKELETON

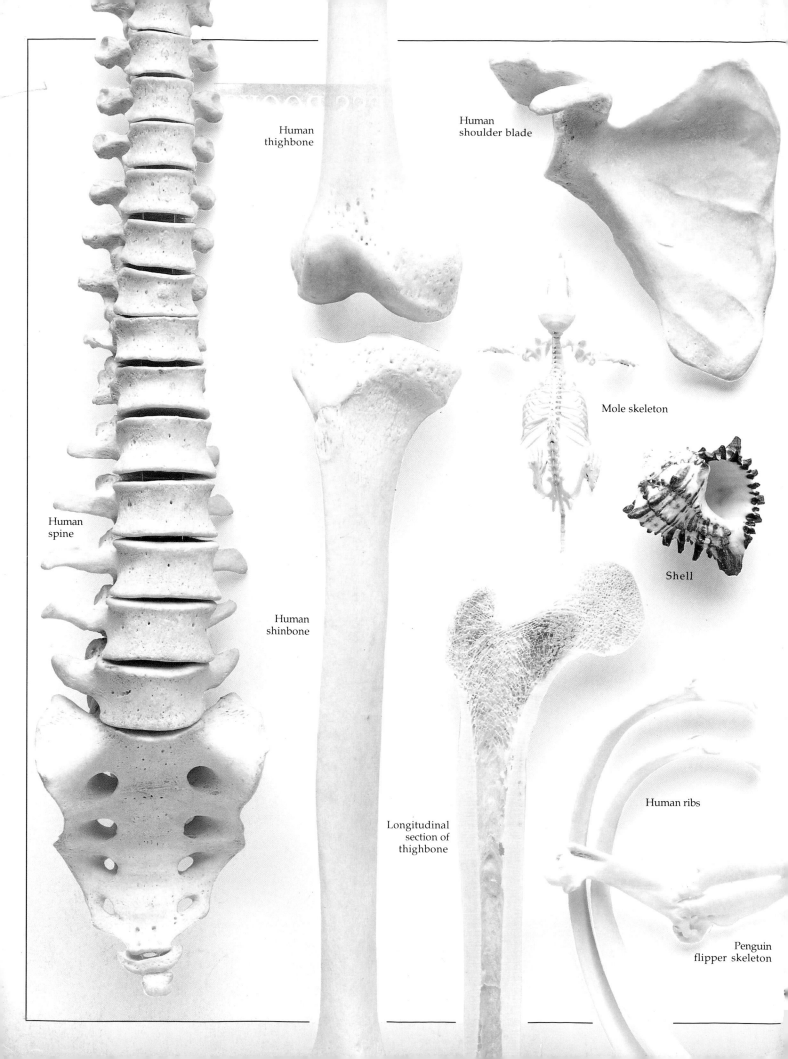

Human
thighbone

Human
shoulder blade

Human
spine

Mole skeleton

Shell

Human
shinbone

Human ribs

Longitudinal
section of
thighbone

Penguin
flipper skeleton

Human
molars

EYEWITNESS BOOKS

Star shell

SKELETON

Written by
STEVE PARKER

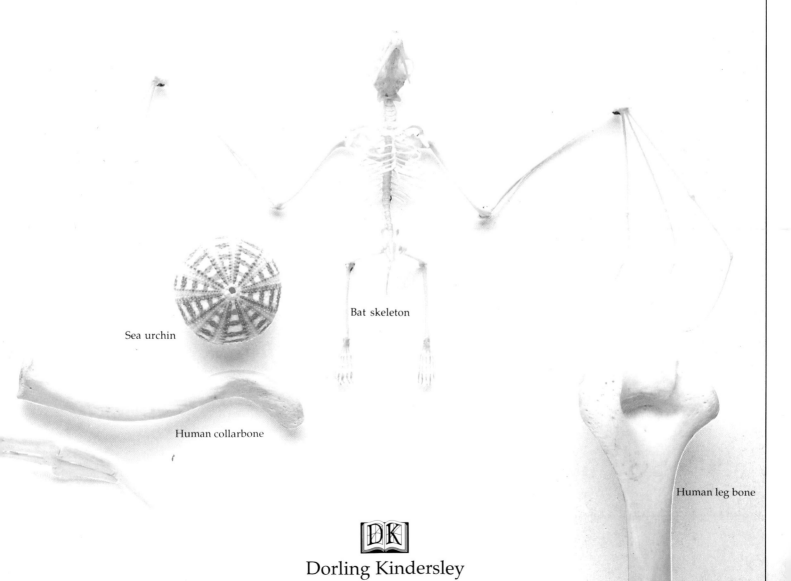

Sea urchin

Bat skeleton

Human collarbone

Human leg bone

Dorling Kindersley

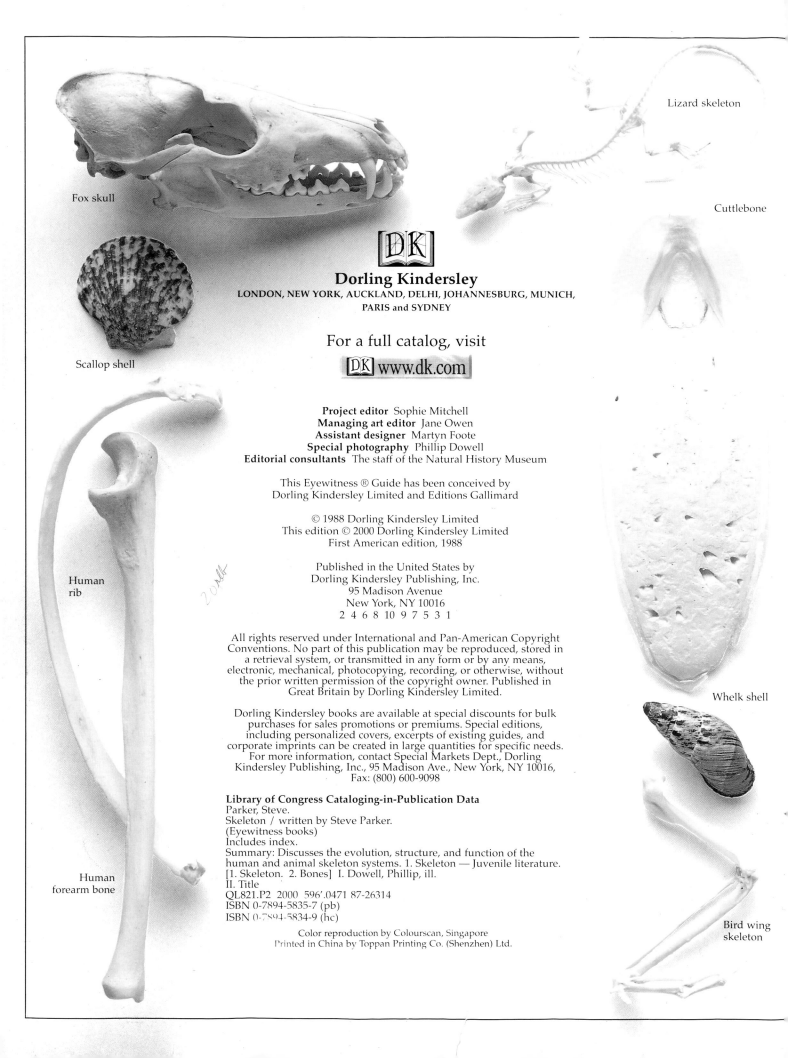

Fox skull

Lizard skeleton

Cuttlebone

Scallop shell

DK

Dorling Kindersley
LONDON, NEW YORK, AUCKLAND, DELHI, JOHANNESBURG, MUNICH, PARIS and SYDNEY

For a full catalog, visit
DK www.dk.com

Project editor Sophie Mitchell
Managing art editor Jane Owen
Assistant designer Martyn Foote
Special photography Phillip Dowell
Editorial consultants The staff of the Natural History Museum

This Eyewitness ® Guide has been conceived by
Dorling Kindersley Limited and Editions Gallimard

© 1988 Dorling Kindersley Limited
This edition © 2000 Dorling Kindersley Limited
First American edition, 1988

Published in the United States by
Dorling Kindersley Publishing, Inc.
95 Madison Avenue
New York, NY 10016
2 4 6 8 10 9 7 5 3 1

Dorling Kindersley books are available at special discounts for bulk
purchases for sales promotions or premiums. Special editions,
including personalized covers, excerpts of existing guides, and
corporate imprints can be created in large quantities for specific needs.
For more information, contact Special Markets Dept., Dorling
Kindersley Publishing, Inc., 95 Madison Ave., New York, NY 10016,
Fax: (800) 600-9098

Library of Congress Cataloging-in-Publication Data
Parker, Steve.
Skeleton / written by Steve Parker.
(Eyewitness books)
Includes index.
Summary: Discusses the evolution, structure, and function of the
human and animal skeleton systems. 1. Skeleton — Juvenile literature.
[1. Skeleton. 2. Bones] I. Dowell, Phillip, ill.
II. Title
QL821.P2 2000 596'.0471 87-26314
ISBN 0-7894-5835-7 (pb)
ISBN 0-7894-5834-9 (hc)

Color reproduction by Colourscan, Singapore
Printed in China by Toppan Printing Co. (Shenzhen) Ltd.

Human
rib

Human
forearm bone

Whelk shell

Bird wing
skeleton

Contents

Crow skull

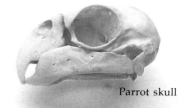

Parrot skull

The human skeleton

A SKELETON IS MANY THINGS: symbol of danger and death, a key that opens any door, a secret kept in a closet, the outline of a novel or grand plan . . . and the 200-odd bones that hold up each human body. Our skeleton supports, moves and protects. It is both rigid and flexible. Individual bones are stiff and unyielding, forming an internal framework that supports the rest of the body and stops it collapsing into a jelly-like heap. Bones together, linked by movable joints and worked by muscles, form a system of girders, levers and pincers that can pick pick an apple from a tree or move the body forward at 20 mph (32 kph). The skeleton protects our most delicate and important organs: the skull shields the brain, and the ribs guard the heart and lungs. The human skeleton follows the basic design found in the 40,000 or so species of backboned animals. But the endless variety of animals has a correspondingly endless variety of skeletons, as this book sets out to show.

BIG HEAD
In relation to body size, the human skull houses one of the biggest brains in the animal world (p. 26).

EARLY IMPRESSION *above*
Medical textbooks of the 18th and 19th centuries would have contained detailed illustrations such as this.

ANATOMY LECTURE *below*
A medieval lecture theater populated by human and animal skeletons.

MEDIEVAL MEDICINE
The surgeon points out details of the rib cage to a 15th-century student.

FOOD PROCESSORS
Human teeth chop their way through about 500 kg (half a ton) of food each year (p. 27).

MEASURING THE SKULL
The craniometer, a device for measuring skull size - and, by deduction, brain size.

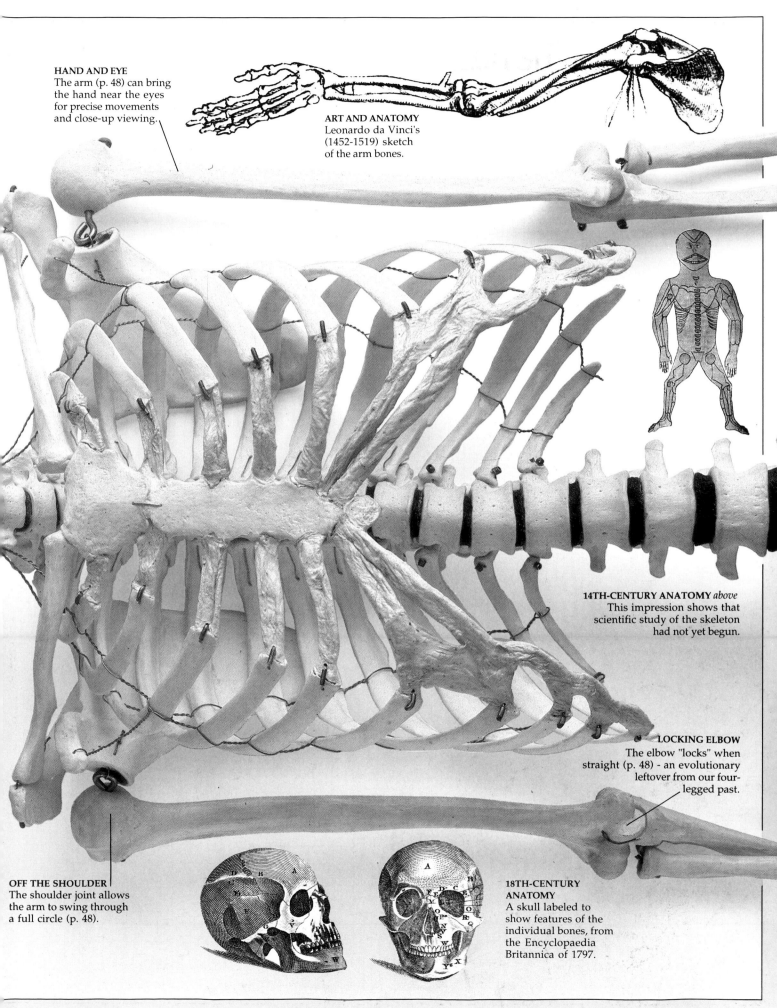

HAND AND EYE
The arm (p. 48) can bring the hand near the eyes for precise movements and close-up viewing.

ART AND ANATOMY
Leonardo da Vinci's (1452-1519) sketch of the arm bones.

14TH-CENTURY ANATOMY *above*
This impression shows that scientific study of the skeleton had not yet begun.

LOCKING ELBOW
The elbow "locks" when straight (p. 48) - an evolutionary leftover from our four-legged past.

OFF THE SHOULDER
The shoulder joint allows the arm to swing through a full circle (p. 48).

18TH-CENTURY ANATOMY
A skull labeled to show features of the individual bones, from the Encyclopaedia Britannica of 1797.

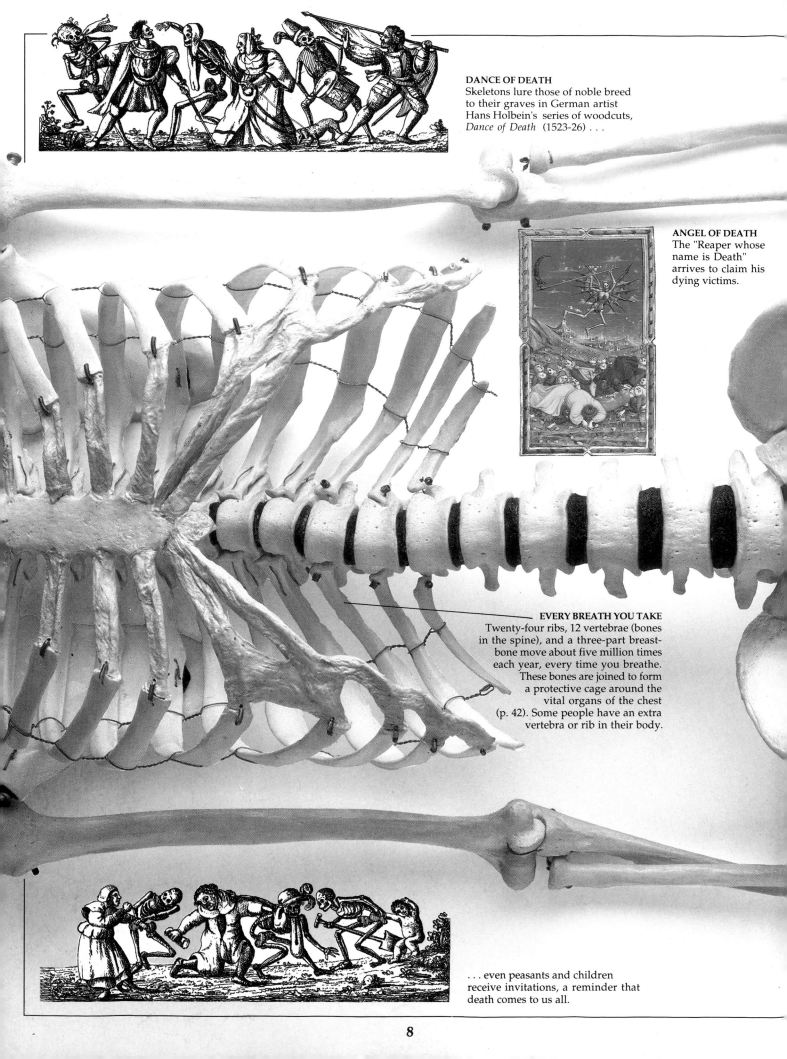

DANCE OF DEATH
Skeletons lure those of noble breed to their graves in German artist Hans Holbein's series of woodcuts, *Dance of Death* (1523-26) . . .

ANGEL OF DEATH
The "Reaper whose name is Death" arrives to claim his dying victims.

EVERY BREATH YOU TAKE
Twenty-four ribs, 12 vertebrae (bones in the spine), and a three-part breastbone move about five million times each year, every time you breathe. These bones are joined to form a protective cage around the vital organs of the chest (p. 42). Some people have an extra vertebra or rib in their body.

. . . even peasants and children receive invitations, a reminder that death comes to us all.

THE UPRIGHT APE
Our close relatives, the monkeys and other apes, move occasionally on two legs. But only the human hip bone is adapted for fully upright, two-legged walking, with legs and spine in a straight line (p. 44).

SAFE-KEEPING
A 14th-century reliquary keeps safe the bones of a saint for Judgment Day.

PIRATE SAILOR
This 18th-century "sailor of fortune" sports the skull and crossbones, piratical symbol of death and destruction.

SYMBOL OF THE END
The skull and bone of the classical "bone" shape (in this case a thigh bone), enduring symbol for the end of life.

FLEXIBLE HANDS
Each hand has 27 bones, and as many joints (p. 49). The human hand can be brought into almost any position in relation to the body through rotation at the shoulder (p. 48) and movements of the forearm and wrist bones.

FORECASTING THE FUTURE
Tarot cards, the oldest playing cards in use today, are supposed to reveal the future. In this case, the future is very short.

XIII

LA MORT

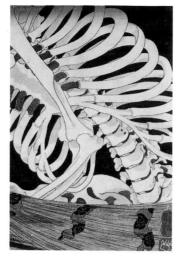

EASTERN MAGIC
Mitsukuni, a Japanese sorceress, summons up a giant skeleton to frighten her enemies in this painting by Kuniyoshi.

THE LONGEST BONES
The bones in the leg are the longest in the human body (p. 54). The leg bones are shaped to allow their lower ends - at the ankles and knees - to touch, while the tops of the thigh bones - at the hip - may be more than 1 ft (30 cm) apart.

MARKING TIME *left*
The seconds tick by for this silver skull - it is the case for a watch, made in Germany in about 1620.

Detail of distorted skull shown in the painting on the right

ARTIST'S ILLUSION
Hans Holbein's *The Ambassadors* (1533) records the opulence of Henry VIII's court;

the odd shape in the foreground is a distorted skull, seen more clearly from one side and very close. (The name Holbein can be translated as "hollow bone".)

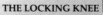

THE LOCKING KNEE
The knee is the largest joint in the body (p. 54), carrying as it does almost half the body's weight. It forms a locking hinge that bends in one direction only.

ALAS, POOR YORICK . . .
Shakespeare's Hamlet (portrayed by a French actor) ponders the skull of the Danish court jester Yorick: "That skull had a tongue in it, and could sing once . . ."

SKULL CUP
The holy lamas (priests) of Tibet use ceremonial cups like this, made from the top of a human skull, symbol of consuming the mind of another.

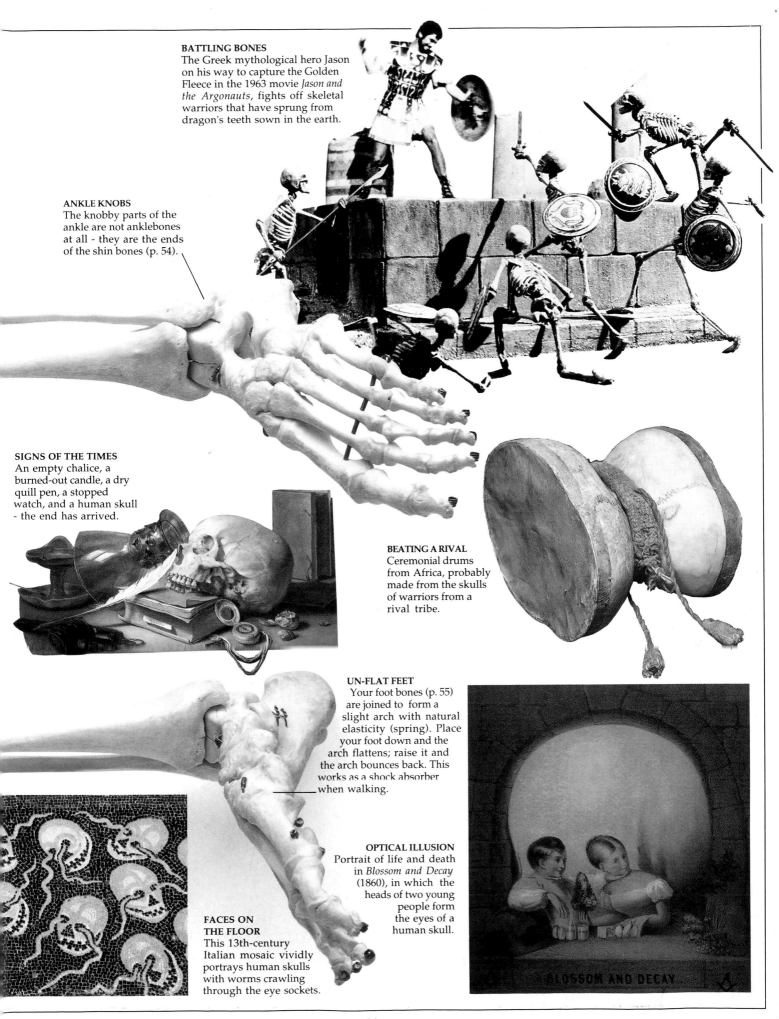

BATTLING BONES
The Greek mythological hero Jason on his way to capture the Golden Fleece in the 1963 movie *Jason and the Argonauts*, fights off skeletal warriors that have sprung from dragon's teeth sown in the earth.

ANKLE KNOBS
The knobby parts of the ankle are not anklebones at all - they are the ends of the shin bones (p. 54).

SIGNS OF THE TIMES
An empty chalice, a burned-out candle, a dry quill pen, a stopped watch, and a human skull - the end has arrived.

BEATING A RIVAL
Ceremonial drums from Africa, probably made from the skulls of warriors from a rival tribe.

UN-FLAT FEET
Your foot bones (p. 55) are joined to form a slight arch with natural elasticity (spring). Place your foot down and the arch flattens; raise it and the arch bounces back. This works as a shock absorber when walking.

OPTICAL ILLUSION
Portrait of life and death in *Blossom and Decay* (1860), in which the heads of two young people form the eyes of a human skull.

FACES ON THE FLOOR
This 13th-century Italian mosaic vividly portrays human skulls with worms crawling through the eye sockets.

BLOSSOM AND DECAY

From bone to stone

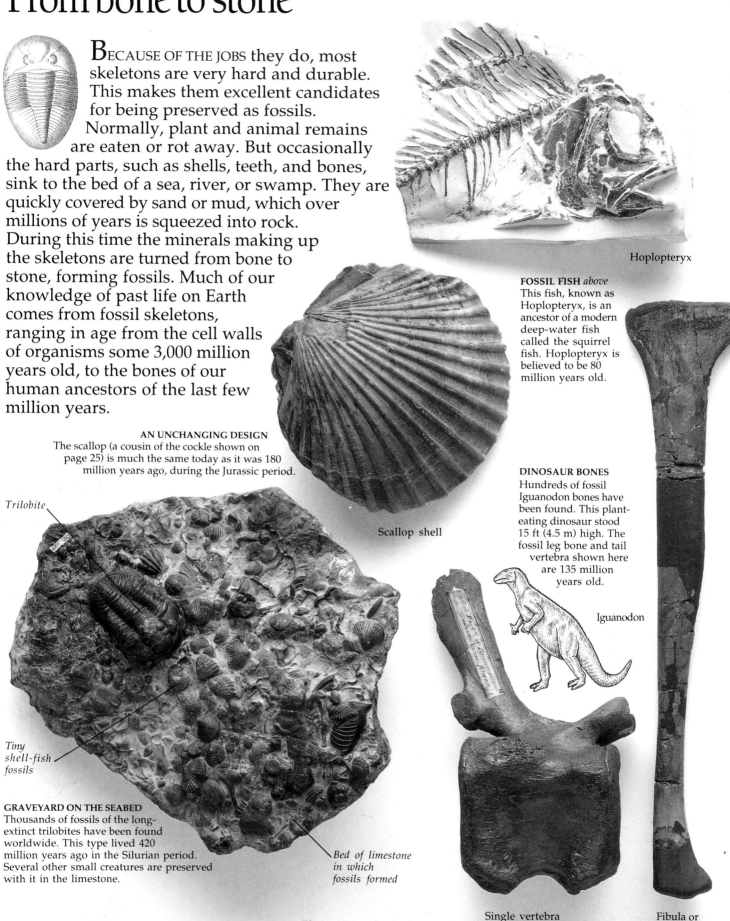

BECAUSE OF THE JOBS they do, most skeletons are very hard and durable. This makes them excellent candidates for being preserved as fossils. Normally, plant and animal remains are eaten or rot away. But occasionally the hard parts, such as shells, teeth, and bones, sink to the bed of a sea, river, or swamp. They are quickly covered by sand or mud, which over millions of years is squeezed into rock. During this time the minerals making up the skeletons are turned from bone to stone, forming fossils. Much of our knowledge of past life on Earth comes from fossil skeletons, ranging in age from the cell walls of organisms some 3,000 million years old, to the bones of our human ancestors of the last few million years.

AN UNCHANGING DESIGN
The scallop (a cousin of the cockle shown on page 25) is much the same today as it was 180 million years ago, during the Jurassic period.

Hoplopteryx

FOSSIL FISH *above*
This fish, known as Hoplopteryx, is an ancestor of a modern deep-water fish called the squirrel fish. Hoplopteryx is believed to be 80 million years old.

Scallop shell

DINOSAUR BONES
Hundreds of fossil Iguanodon bones have been found. This plant-eating dinosaur stood 15 ft (4.5 m) high. The fossil leg bone and tail vertebra shown here are 135 million years old.

Iguanodon

Trilobite

Tiny shell-fish fossils

GRAVEYARD ON THE SEABED
Thousands of fossils of the long-extinct trilobites have been found worldwide. This type lived 420 million years ago in the Silurian period. Several other small creatures are preserved with it in the limestone.

Bed of limestone in which fossils formed

Single vertebra from the dinosaur's tail

Fibula or lower leg bone

12

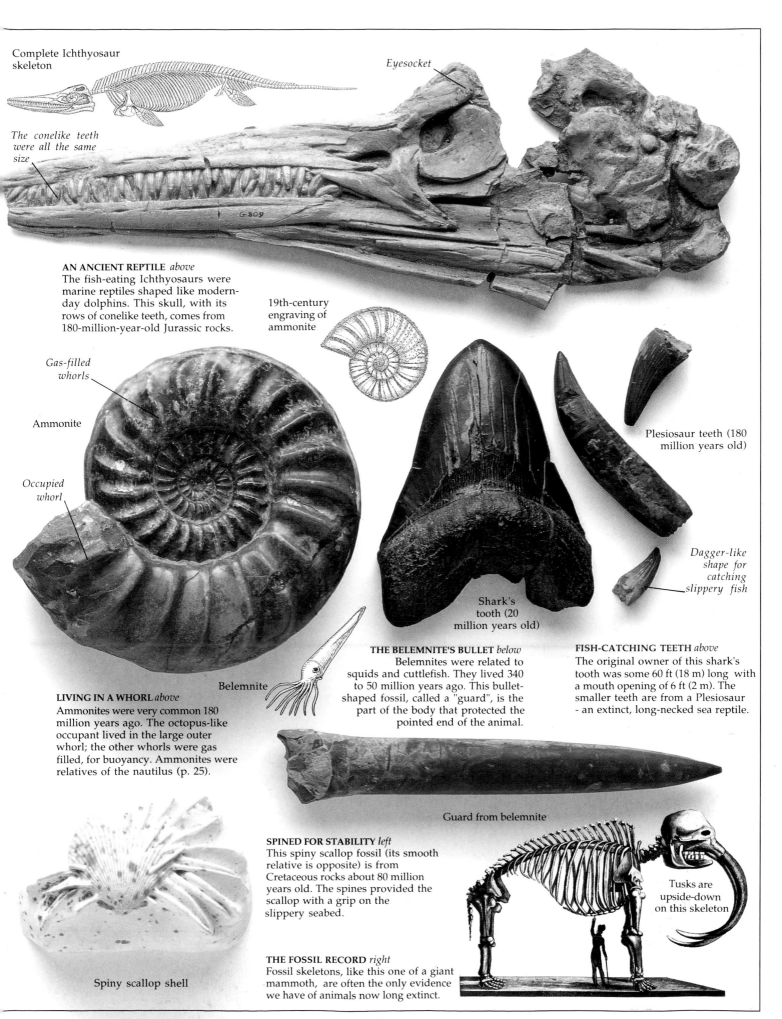

Complete Ichthyosaur skeleton

The conelike teeth were all the same size

Eyesocket

AN ANCIENT REPTILE *above*
The fish-eating Ichthyosaurs were marine reptiles shaped like modern-day dolphins. This skull, with its rows of conelike teeth, comes from 180-million-year-old Jurassic rocks.

19th-century engraving of ammonite

Gas-filled whorls

Ammonite

Occupied whorl

Plesiosaur teeth (180 million years old)

Dagger-like shape for catching slippery fish

Shark's tooth (20 million years old)

Belemnite

THE BELEMNITE'S BULLET *below*
Belemnites were related to squids and cuttlefish. They lived 340 to 50 million years ago. This bullet-shaped fossil, called a "guard", is the part of the body that protected the pointed end of the animal.

FISH-CATCHING TEETH *above*
The original owner of this shark's tooth was some 60 ft (18 m) long with a mouth opening of 6 ft (2 m). The smaller teeth are from a Plesiosaur - an extinct, long-necked sea reptile.

LIVING IN A WHORL *above*
Ammonites were very common 180 million years ago. The octopus-like occupant lived in the large outer whorl; the other whorls were gas filled, for buoyancy. Ammonites were relatives of the nautilus (p. 25).

Guard from belemnite

SPINED FOR STABILITY *left*
This spiny scallop fossil (its smooth relative is opposite) is from Cretaceous rocks about 80 million years old. The spines provided the scallop with a grip on the slippery seabed.

Tusks are upside-down on this skeleton

THE FOSSIL RECORD *right*
Fossil skeletons, like this one of a giant mammoth, are often the only evidence we have of animals now long extinct.

Spiny scallop shell

13

Mammals

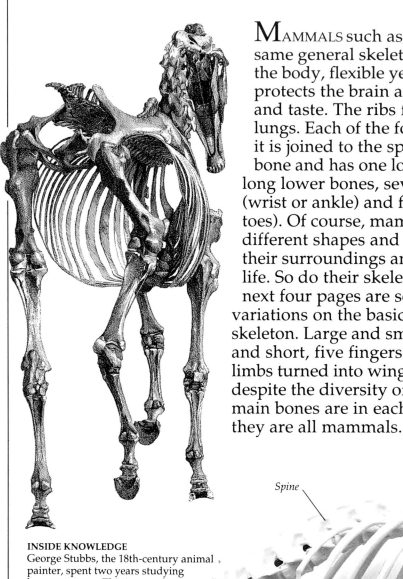

MAMMALS such as dogs, cats, monkeys, and humans all have the same general skeleton design. The spine is the main support for the body, flexible yet able to be held rigid. The skull houses and protects the brain and the delicate organs of sight, hearing, smell, and taste. The ribs form a protective cage around the heart and lungs. Each of the four limbs is basically the same: it is joined to the spine via a flat, broad bone and has one long upper bone, two long lower bones, several smaller bones (wrist or ankle) and five digits (fingers or toes). Of course, mammals come in different shapes and sizes, adapted to their surroundings and way of life. So do their skeletons. On the next four pages are some of the many variations on the basic mammalian skeleton. Large and small, long limbs and short, five fingers or fewer, front limbs turned into wings or paddles - despite the diversity of design, the same main bones are in each creature, and they are all mammals.

Many of the larger mammals are now extinct, like this mammoth

INSIDE KNOWLEDGE
George Stubbs, the 18th-century animal painter, spent two years studying horse anatomy. This is one of his drawings of a horse skeleton, done in 1766.

Spine

Hip bone

Rib cage

Badger skeleton

Hind limbs are at an angle giving badger its distinctive posture

Tail vertebrae

THE BADGER'S DESIGN FOR DIGGING
The squat, powerfully built badger is not known for its fleetness of foot. Its thick-boned limbs, strong feet and long claws are designed for digging tunnels and scratching into the earth for small creatures to eat. Its teeth are those of a meat eater (p. 36), although the badger eats berries and other plant food too.

Toes have claws for digging up soil

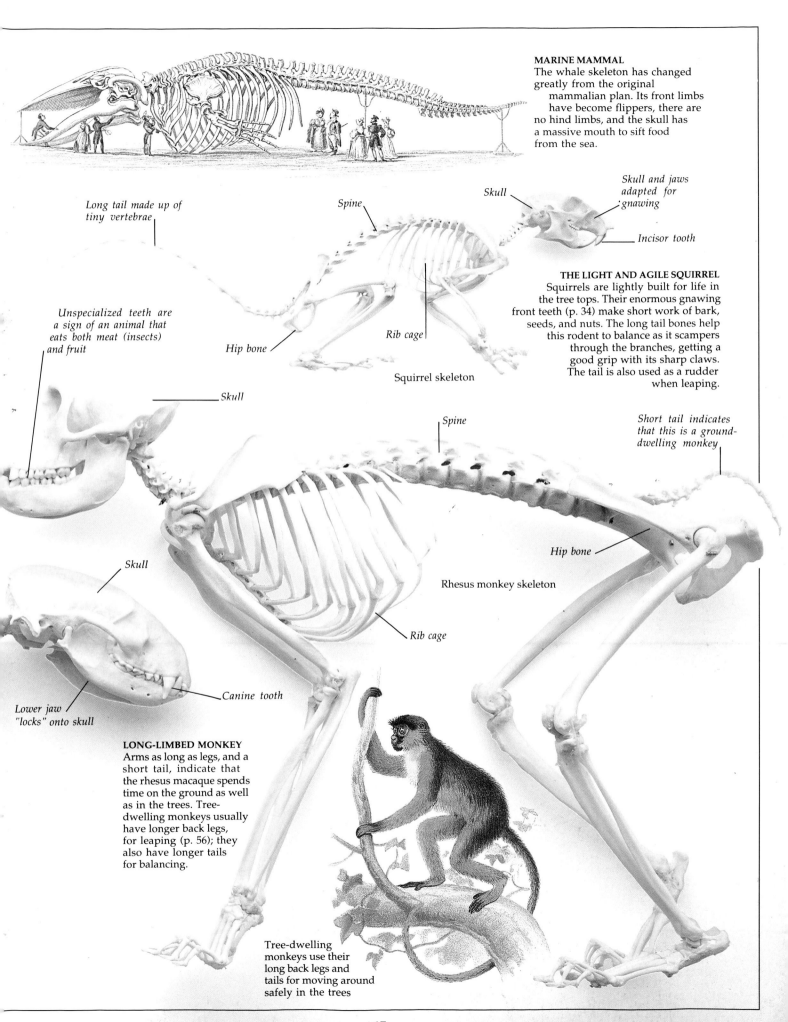

MARINE MAMMAL
The whale skeleton has changed greatly from the original mammalian plan. Its front limbs have become flippers, there are no hind limbs, and the skull has a massive mouth to sift food from the sea.

Long tail made up of tiny vertebrae

Spine

Skull

Skull and jaws adapted for gnawing

Incisor tooth

THE LIGHT AND AGILE SQUIRREL
Squirrels are lightly built for life in the tree tops. Their enormous gnawing front teeth (p. 34) make short work of bark, seeds, and nuts. The long tail bones help this rodent to balance as it scampers through the branches, getting a good grip with its sharp claws. The tail is also used as a rudder when leaping.

Unspecialized teeth are a sign of an animal that eats both meat (insects) and fruit

Hip bone

Rib cage

Squirrel skeleton

Skull

Spine

Short tail indicates that this is a ground-dwelling monkey

Rhesus monkey skeleton

Hip bone

Skull

Rib cage

Canine tooth

Lower jaw "locks" onto skull

LONG-LIMBED MONKEY
Arms as long as legs, and a short tail, indicate that the rhesus macaque spends time on the ground as well as in the trees. Tree-dwelling monkeys usually have longer back legs, for leaping (p. 56); they also have longer tails for balancing.

Tree-dwelling monkeys use their long back legs and tails for moving around safely in the trees

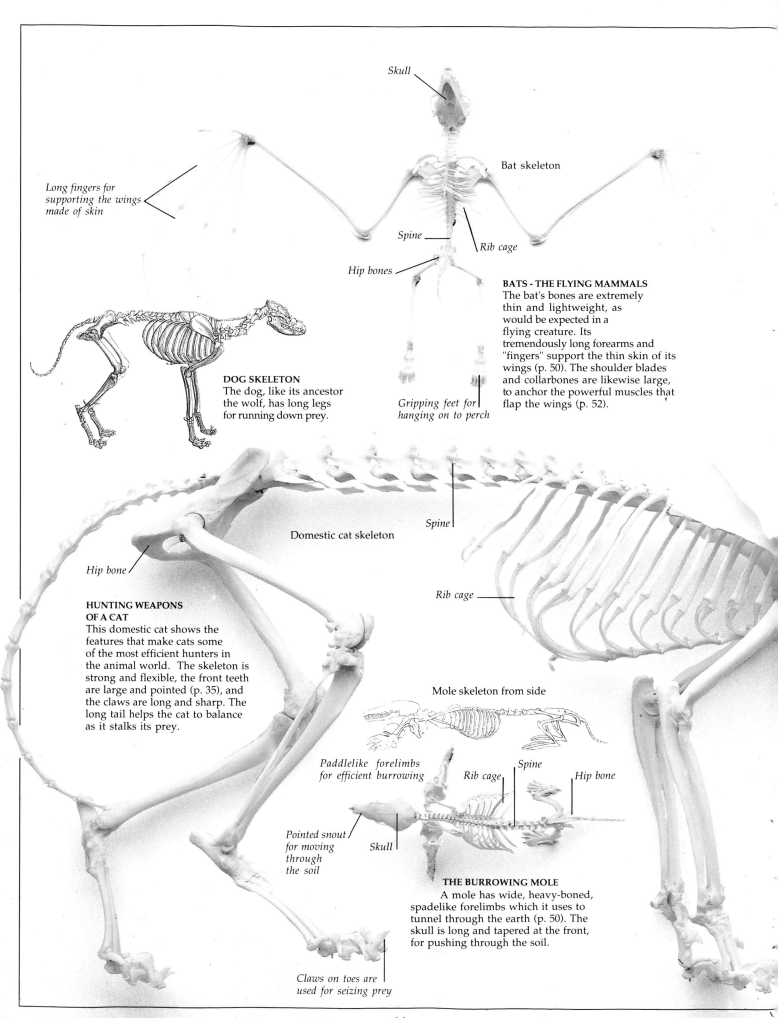

Skull

Bat skeleton

Long fingers for supporting the wings made of skin

Spine

Rib cage

Hip bones

BATS - THE FLYING MAMMALS
The bat's bones are extremely thin and lightweight, as would be expected in a flying creature. Its tremendously long forearms and "fingers" support the thin skin of its wings (p. 50). The shoulder blades and collarbones are likewise large, to anchor the powerful muscles that flap the wings (p. 52).

Gripping feet for hanging on to perch

DOG SKELETON
The dog, like its ancestor the wolf, has long legs for running down prey.

Spine

Domestic cat skeleton

Hip bone

HUNTING WEAPONS OF A CAT
This domestic cat shows the features that make cats some of the most efficient hunters in the animal world. The skeleton is strong and flexible, the front teeth are large and pointed (p. 35), and the claws are long and sharp. The long tail helps the cat to balance as it stalks its prey.

Rib cage

Mole skeleton from side

Paddlelike forelimbs for efficient burrowing

Spine

Rib cage

Hip bone

Pointed snout for moving through the soil

Skull

THE BURROWING MOLE
A mole has wide, heavy-boned, spadelike forelimbs which it uses to tunnel through the earth (p. 50). The skull is long and tapered at the front, for pushing through the soil.

Claws on toes are used for seizing prey

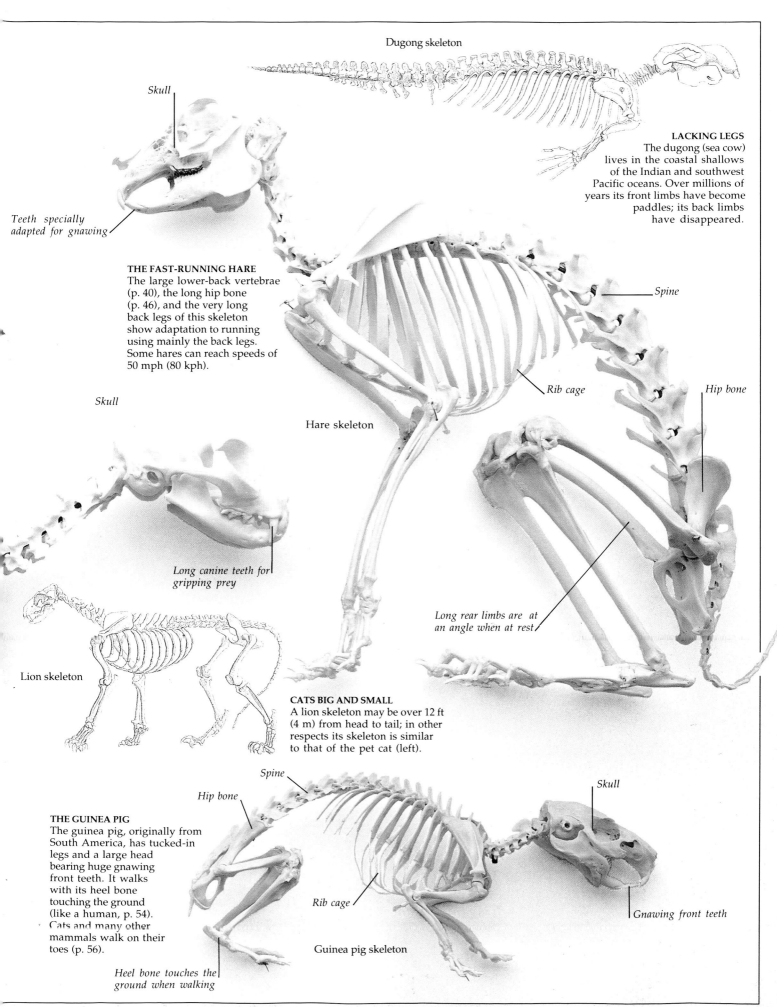

Dugong skeleton

Skull

Teeth specially adapted for gnawing

LACKING LEGS
The dugong (sea cow) lives in the coastal shallows of the Indian and southwest Pacific oceans. Over millions of years its front limbs have become paddles; its back limbs have disappeared.

THE FAST-RUNNING HARE
The large lower-back vertebrae (p. 40), the long hip bone (p. 46), and the very long back legs of this skeleton show adaptation to running using mainly the back legs. Some hares can reach speeds of 50 mph (80 kph).

Spine

Skull

Rib cage

Hip bone

Hare skeleton

Long canine teeth for gripping prey

Long rear limbs are at an angle when at rest

Lion skeleton

CATS BIG AND SMALL
A lion skeleton may be over 12 ft (4 m) from head to tail; in other respects its skeleton is similar to that of the pet cat (left).

Spine

Hip bone

Skull

THE GUINEA PIG
The guinea pig, originally from South America, has tucked-in legs and a large head bearing huge gnawing front teeth. It walks with its heel bone touching the ground (like a human, p. 54). Cats and many other mammals walk on their toes (p. 56).

Rib cage

Gnawing front teeth

Guinea pig skeleton

Heel bone touches the ground when walking

Birds

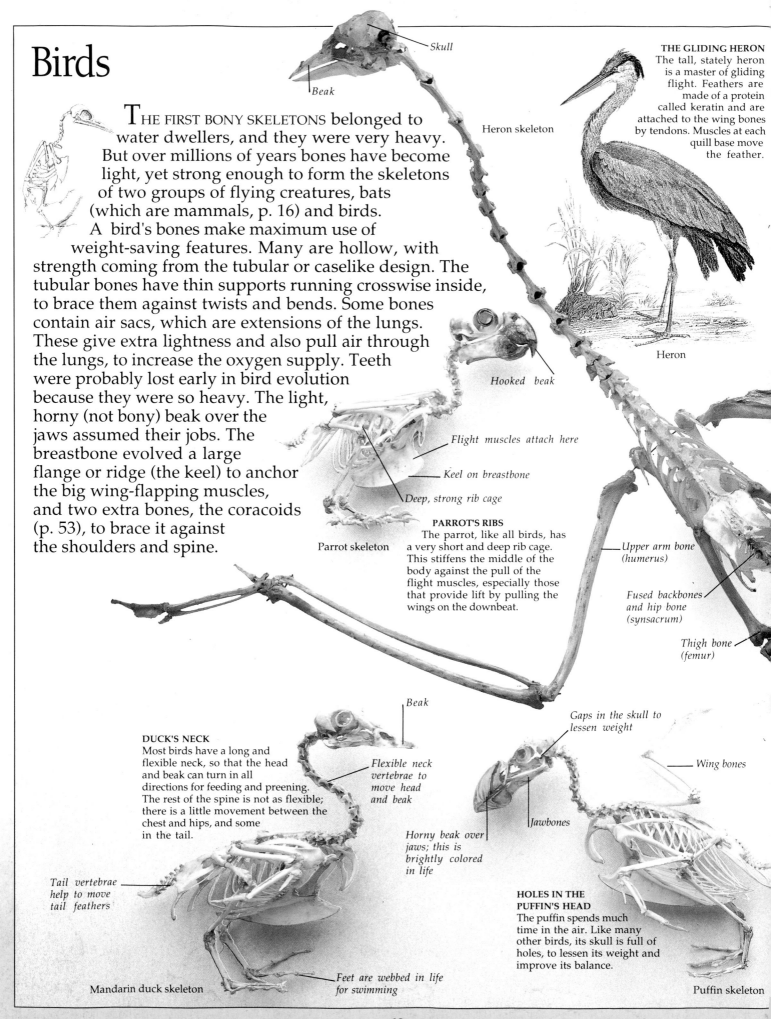

THE FIRST BONY SKELETONS belonged to water dwellers, and they were very heavy. But over millions of years bones have become light, yet strong enough to form the skeletons of two groups of flying creatures, bats (which are mammals, p. 16) and birds.

A bird's bones make maximum use of weight-saving features. Many are hollow, with strength coming from the tubular or caselike design. The tubular bones have thin supports running crosswise inside, to brace them against twists and bends. Some bones contain air sacs, which are extensions of the lungs. These give extra lightness and also pull air through the lungs, to increase the oxygen supply. Teeth were probably lost early in bird evolution because they were so heavy. The light, horny (not bony) beak over the jaws assumed their jobs. The breastbone evolved a large flange or ridge (the keel) to anchor the big wing-flapping muscles, and two extra bones, the coracoids (p. 53), to brace it against the shoulders and spine.

Skull

Beak

Heron skeleton

THE GLIDING HERON
The tall, stately heron is a master of gliding flight. Feathers are made of a protein called keratin and are attached to the wing bones by tendons. Muscles at each quill base move the feather.

Heron

Hooked beak

Flight muscles attach here

Keel on breastbone

Deep, strong rib cage

PARROT'S RIBS
The parrot, like all birds, has a very short and deep rib cage. This stiffens the middle of the body against the pull of the flight muscles, especially those that provide lift by pulling the wings on the downbeat.

Parrot skeleton

Upper arm bone (humerus)

Fused backbones and hip bone (synsacrum)

Thigh bone (femur)

Beak

DUCK'S NECK
Most birds have a long and flexible neck, so that the head and beak can turn in all directions for feeding and preening. The rest of the spine is not as flexible; there is a little movement between the chest and hips, and some in the tail.

Flexible neck vertebrae to move head and beak

Gaps in the skull to lessen weight

Wing bones

Jawbones

Horny beak over jaws; this is brightly colored in life

Tail vertebrae help to move tail feathers

HOLES IN THE PUFFIN'S HEAD
The puffin spends much time in the air. Like many other birds, its skull is full of holes, to lessen its weight and improve its balance.

Feet are webbed in life for swimming

Mandarin duck skeleton

Puffin skeleton

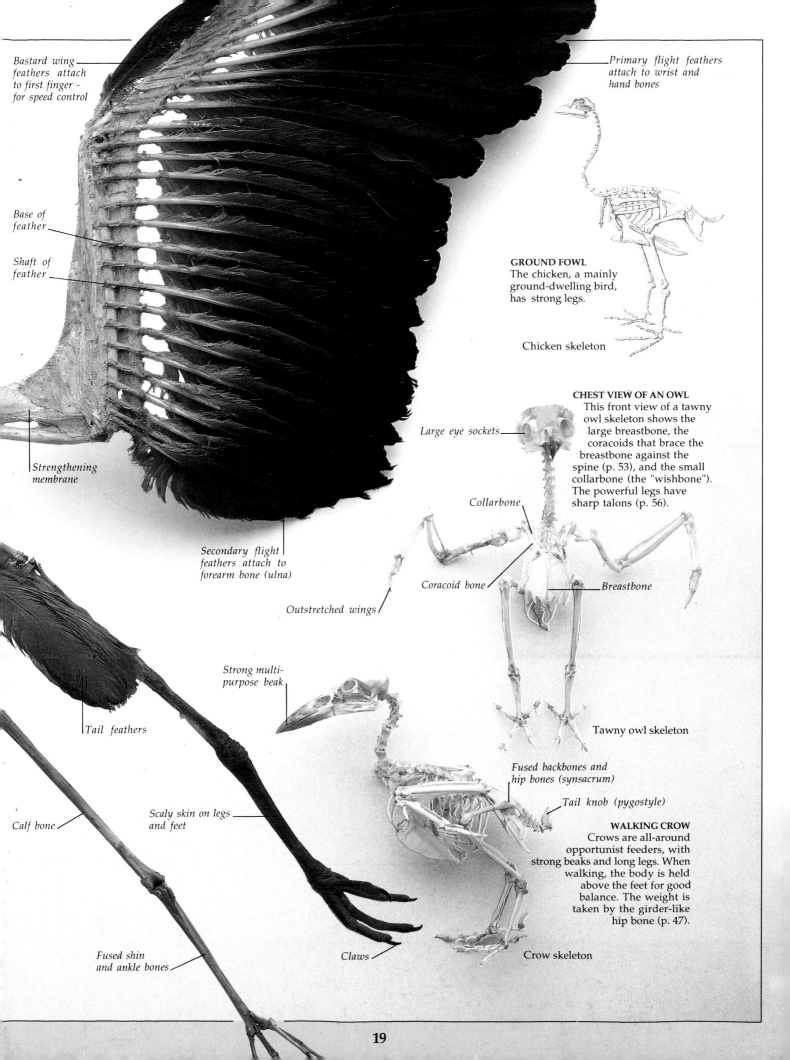

Bastard wing feathers attach to first finger - for speed control

Primary flight feathers attach to wrist and hand bones

Base of feather

Shaft of feather

Strengthening membrane

GROUND FOWL
The chicken, a mainly ground-dwelling bird, has strong legs.

Chicken skeleton

CHEST VIEW OF AN OWL
This front view of a tawny owl skeleton shows the large breastbone, the coracoids that brace the breastbone against the spine (p. 53), and the small collarbone (the "wishbone"). The powerful legs have sharp talons (p. 56).

Large eye sockets

Collarbone

Coracoid bone

Breastbone

Secondary flight feathers attach to forearm bone (ulna)

Outstretched wings

Tawny owl skeleton

Strong multi-purpose beak

Tail feathers

Fused backbones and hip bones (synsacrum)

Tail knob (pygostyle)

WALKING CROW
Crows are all-around opportunist feeders, with strong beaks and long legs. When walking, the body is held above the feet for good balance. The weight is taken by the girder-like hip bone (p. 47).

Calf bone

Scaly skin on legs and feet

Fused shin and ankle bones

Claws

Crow skeleton

Fish, reptiles, and amphibians

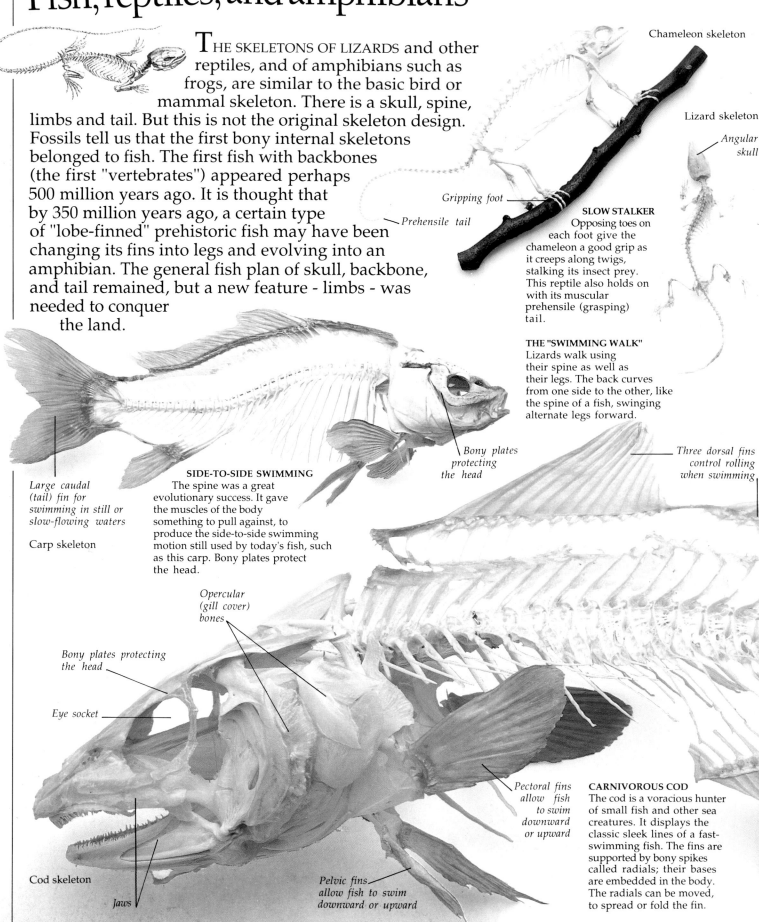

THE SKELETONS OF LIZARDS and other reptiles, and of amphibians such as frogs, are similar to the basic bird or mammal skeleton. There is a skull, spine, limbs and tail. But this is not the original skeleton design. Fossils tell us that the first bony internal skeletons belonged to fish. The first fish with backbones (the first "vertebrates") appeared perhaps 500 million years ago. It is thought that by 350 million years ago, a certain type of "lobe-finned" prehistoric fish may have been changing its fins into legs and evolving into an amphibian. The general fish plan of skull, backbone, and tail remained, but a new feature - limbs - was needed to conquer the land.

Chameleon skeleton

Lizard skeleton

Angular skull

Gripping foot

Prehensile tail

SLOW STALKER
Opposing toes on each foot give the chameleon a good grip as it creeps along twigs, stalking its insect prey. This reptile also holds on with its muscular prehensile (grasping) tail.

THE "SWIMMING WALK"
Lizards walk using their spine as well as their legs. The back curves from one side to the other, like the spine of a fish, swinging alternate legs forward.

Bony plates protecting the head

Three dorsal fins control rolling when swimming

Large caudal (tail) fin for swimming in still or slow-flowing waters

Carp skeleton

SIDE-TO-SIDE SWIMMING
The spine was a great evolutionary success. It gave the muscles of the body something to pull against, to produce the side-to-side swimming motion still used by today's fish, such as this carp. Bony plates protect the head.

Opercular (gill cover) bones

Bony plates protecting the head

Eye socket

Cod skeleton

Jaws

Pelvic fins allow fish to swim downward or upward

Pectoral fins allow fish to swim downward or upward

CARNIVOROUS COD
The cod is a voracious hunter of small fish and other sea creatures. It displays the classic sleek lines of a fast-swimming fish. The fins are supported by bony spikes called radials; their bases are embedded in the body. The radials can be moved, to spread or fold the fin.

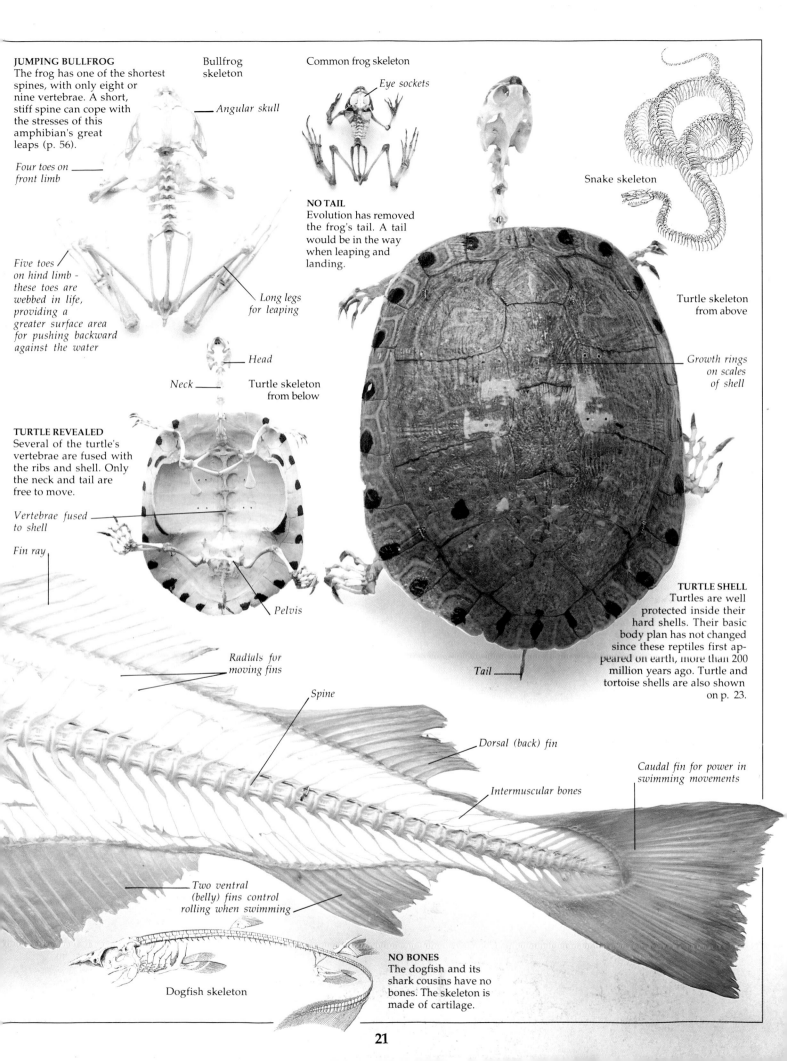

JUMPING BULLFROG
The frog has one of the shortest spines, with only eight or nine vertebrae. A short, stiff spine can cope with the stresses of this amphibian's great leaps (p. 56).

Bullfrog skeleton

Common frog skeleton

Angular skull

Eye sockets

Four toes on front limb

Snake skeleton

Five toes on hind limb - these toes are webbed in life, providing a greater surface area for pushing backward against the water

NO TAIL
Evolution has removed the frog's tail. A tail would be in the way when leaping and landing.

Long legs for leaping

Turtle skeleton from above

Head

Neck

Turtle skeleton from below

Growth rings on scales of shell

TURTLE REVEALED
Several of the turtle's vertebrae are fused with the ribs and shell. Only the neck and tail are free to move.

Vertebrae fused to shell

Fin ray

Pelvis

Radials for moving fins

Spine

TURTLE SHELL
Turtles are well protected inside their hard shells. Their basic body plan has not changed since these reptiles first appeared on earth, more than 200 million years ago. Turtle and tortoise shells are also shown on p. 23.

Tail

Dorsal (back) fin

Intermuscular bones

Caudal fin for power in swimming movements

Two ventral (belly) fins control rolling when swimming

Dogfish skeleton

NO BONES
The dogfish and its shark cousins have no bones. The skeleton is made of cartilage.

Skeletons on the outside

Magnification X40

THE VAST MAJORITY of animals do not have a bony internal skeleton. Insects, spiders, shellfish, and other invertebrates (animals with no backbone) have a hard outer casing called an exoskeleton. This exoskeleton does the same job as an internal skeleton, providing strength and support. It also forms a hard, protective shield around the soft inner organs. But it does have drawbacks. It cannot expand, so the animal must grow by molting (shedding) its old exoskeleton and making a new, larger one. Above a certain size it becomes so thick and heavy that the muscles cannot move it. This is why animals with exoskeletons tend to be small.

MICROSKELETONS
Diatoms float by the billions in the oceans. Like plants, these single-celled algae trap the sun's light energy to grow. They construct silica casings around themselves, presumably for protection. These "skeletons" are amazingly elaborate and beautiful in shape and variety.

WOOD-BORING BEETLE
This metallic purple and yellow beetle has a larva that bores under the bark of trees.

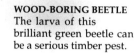

WOOD-BORING BEETLE
Larvae of this wood borer can live up to 30 years.

WOOD-BORING BEETLE
The larva of this brilliant green beetle can be a serious timber pest.

LEAF BEETLE
A brilliant green exoskeleton camouflages these beetles among leaves.

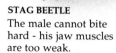

STAG BEETLE
The male cannot bite hard - his jaw muscles are too weak.

DUNG BEETLE
This beetle makes a dung-filled burrow as food for its young.

DARKLING BEETLE
Long antennae help this beetle feel its way around.

ALLOVER ARMOR
Like other insects, beetles are well protected by a tough exoskeleton made of a hard, waterproof material called chitin. The wing cases were once another pair of wings, since modified by evolution. This goliath beetle is the heaviest insect, weighing 3.5 oz (100 g).

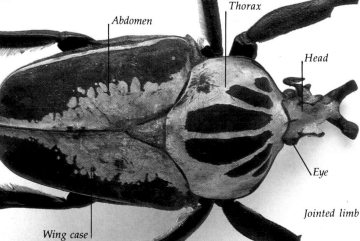

Abdomen

Thorax

Head

Eye

Jointed limb

Wing case

Goliath beetle

Leg muscles are inside tubular leg skeleton

Transparent wing

THE WINGS REVEALED
Under the hard outer wing cases lie the delicate, transparent wings used for flight. The long legs have many joints.

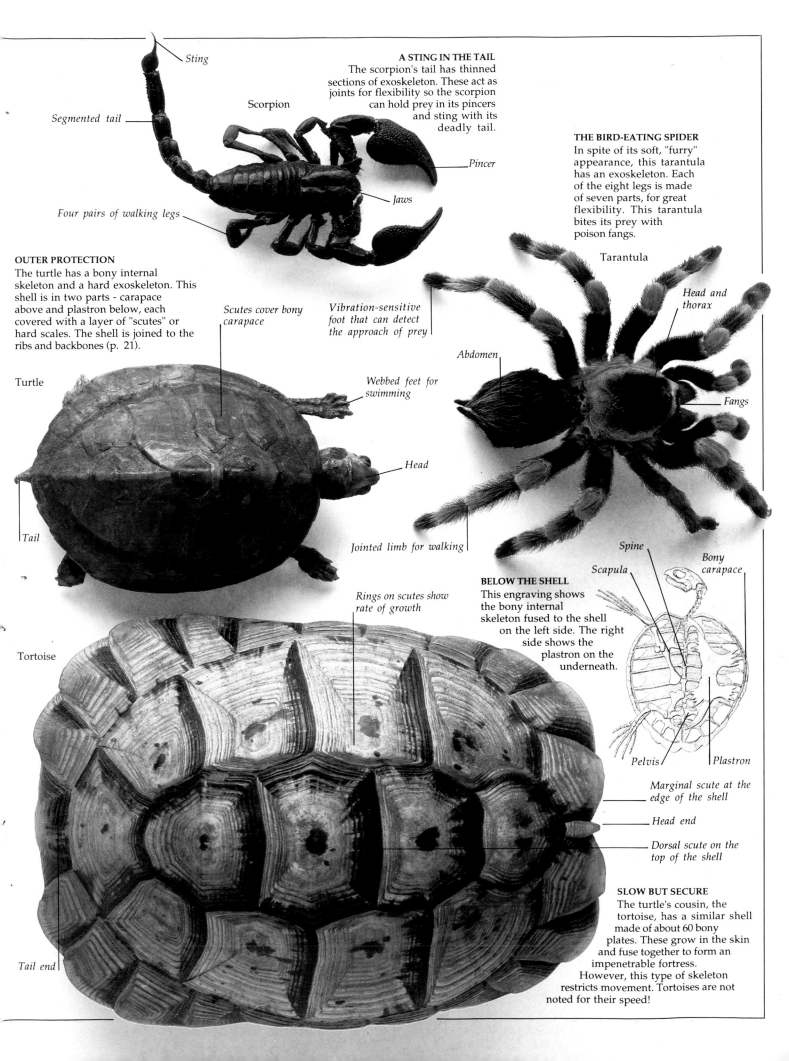

Sting

Segmented tail

Scorpion

A STING IN THE TAIL
The scorpion's tail has thinned sections of exoskeleton. These act as joints for flexibility so the scorpion can hold prey in its pincers and sting with its deadly tail.

THE BIRD-EATING SPIDER
In spite of its soft, "furry" appearance, this tarantula has an exoskeleton. Each of the eight legs is made of seven parts, for great flexibility. This tarantula bites its prey with poison fangs.

Pincer

Jaws

Four pairs of walking legs

OUTER PROTECTION
The turtle has a bony internal skeleton and a hard exoskeleton. This shell is in two parts - carapace above and plastron below, each covered with a layer of "scutes" or hard scales. The shell is joined to the ribs and backbones (p. 21).

Scutes cover bony carapace

Vibration-sensitive foot that can detect the approach of prey

Tarantula

Head and thorax

Abdomen

Fangs

Turtle

Webbed feet for swimming

Head

Tail

Jointed limb for walking

Rings on scutes show rate of growth

Spine

Scapula

Bony carapace

BELOW THE SHELL
This engraving shows the bony internal skeleton fused to the shell on the left side. The right side shows the plastron on the underneath.

Tortoise

Pelvis

Plastron

Marginal scute at the edge of the shell

Head end

Dorsal scute on the top of the shell

SLOW BUT SECURE
The turtle's cousin, the tortoise, has a similar shell made of about 60 bony plates. These grow in the skin and fuse together to form an impenetrable fortress.
However, this type of skeleton restricts movement. Tortoises are not noted for their speed!

Tail end

Marine exoskeletons

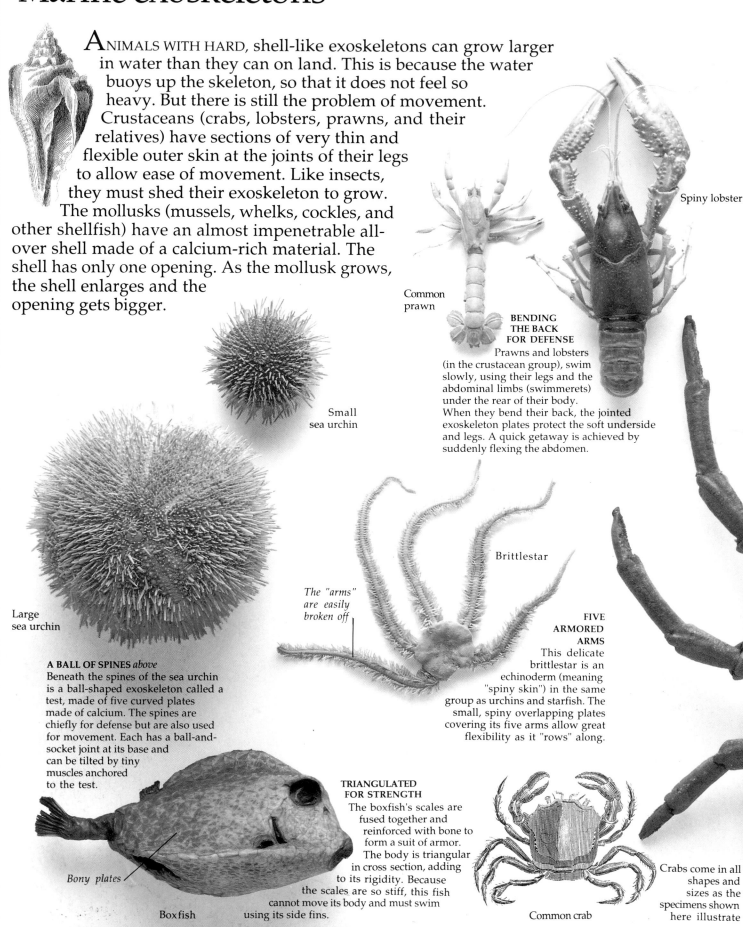

ANIMALS WITH HARD, shell-like exoskeletons can grow larger in water than they can on land. This is because the water buoys up the skeleton, so that it does not feel so heavy. But there is still the problem of movement. Crustaceans (crabs, lobsters, prawns, and their relatives) have sections of very thin and flexible outer skin at the joints of their legs to allow ease of movement. Like insects, they must shed their exoskeleton to grow. The mollusks (mussels, whelks, cockles, and other shellfish) have an almost impenetrable all-over shell made of a calcium-rich material. The shell has only one opening. As the mollusk grows, the shell enlarges and the opening gets bigger.

Spiny lobster

Common prawn

Small sea urchin

BENDING THE BACK FOR DEFENSE
Prawns and lobsters (in the crustacean group), swim slowly, using their legs and the abdominal limbs (swimmerets) under the rear of their body. When they bend their back, the jointed exoskeleton plates protect the soft underside and legs. A quick getaway is achieved by suddenly flexing the abdomen.

Brittlestar

The "arms" are easily broken off

Large sea urchin

A BALL OF SPINES *above*
Beneath the spines of the sea urchin is a ball-shaped exoskeleton called a test, made of five curved plates made of calcium. The spines are chiefly for defense but are also used for movement. Each has a ball-and-socket joint at its base and can be tilted by tiny muscles anchored to the test.

FIVE ARMORED ARMS
This delicate brittlestar is an echinoderm (meaning "spiny skin") in the same group as urchins and starfish. The small, spiny overlapping plates covering its five arms allow great flexibility as it "rows" along.

TRIANGULATED FOR STRENGTH
The boxfish's scales are fused together and reinforced with bone to form a suit of armor. The body is triangular in cross section, adding to its rigidity. Because the scales are so stiff, this fish cannot move its body and must swim using its side fins.

Bony plates

Boxfish

Common crab

Crabs come in all shapes and sizes as the specimens shown here illustrate

Seen upside down, the starfish reveals its central mouth

Starfish

Precious wentletrap

Nautilus

Money cowries

ARMS WITH FEET

Beneath the starfish's arms are small holes. Tiny "tube feet" poke through them. They wave to and fro and have suckers at the ends. The starfish walks using these tube feet; its plated arms are much less flexible.

Masked crab

The ridges on the shell look like a face mask

SEASHORE SHELLS

Mollusks such as the nautilus and the wentletrap have a coiled shell for an outer skeleton. To grow, the animal adds another coil, or whorl. The adult cowrie's whorl wraps around the whole shell.

Entrance to shell

Prickly cockle

A COCKLE'S MUSCLES

The sand-dwelling cockle has a pair of thick, ribbed shells to protect it from the pounding surf and shore rocks. The two shells, or valves, are opened and closed by strong muscles.

Claw

Eye

The exoskeleton has many joints

Spiny spider crab

Seahorse

Prehensile tail

CHANGING SKELETONS

A crab must crawl out of its old exoskeleton when this becomes too small - right down to its last leg and antenna. Quickly the crab's soft body expands, then a fresh exoskeleton hardens over it. The molt takes several hours, during which the vulnerable creature hides in a crack or under a boulder.

Hermit crab

USING CASTOFFS

The hermit crab protects its soft body in a castoff mollusk shell.

BONY OUTER COVERING

The strange-looking seahorse is a true fish, but it swims upright. An armor of bony rings encases its body, and its fins provide movement. The prehensile tail grasps seaweed.

The human skull and teeth

ALTHOUGH THE HEAD is at one end of the human body, it functions as the body's center. The skull protects the brain, which is the central coordinator for receiving information from the outside world and organizing the body's reactions. The special senses of sight, hearing, smell, and taste are concentrated in the skull. In particular, the eyes and inner ears (where the delicate organs of hearing are sited) lie well protected in bony recesses. Air, containing the oxygen vital to life, passes through the skull by way of the nose and mouth. Food is crushed first by the jaws and teeth so that it can be swallowed and digested more easily. The senses of smell and taste are well positioned to check air and food for harmful odors and flavors.

THIS WON'T HURT ...
Teeth are both tough and sensitive. A visit to a medieval dentist was a painful affair, but it would hopefully give merciful relief from long-term nagging toothache.

BRAINCASE
The delicate brain tissue is surrounded by a bony case. Its internal volume is some 2.5 pints (about 1,500 cc).

EYE HOLE
The eye socket, or orbit, protects the eyeball, which is a sphere about 1 in (25 mm) across. The socket is larger; sandwiched between the eyeball and the socket are cushioning pads of fat, nerves, and blood vessels, and the muscles that move the eye.

A COLORED SKULL
A computer-colored x-ray shows the bones in the skull and neck. The soft tissues of the nose, which is not made of bone, also show up.

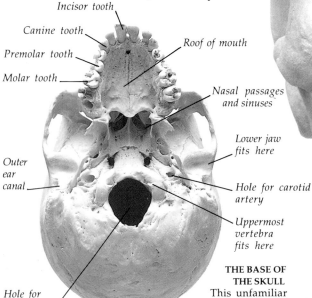

Incisor tooth

Canine tooth

Premolar tooth

Molar tooth

Roof of mouth

Nasal passages and sinuses

Lower jaw fits here

Outer ear canal

Hole for carotid artery

Uppermost vertebra fits here

Hole for spinal cord

THE BASE OF THE SKULL
This unfamiliar underview of the skull, with the lower jaw removed, shows the delicate internal sectioning. (The individual bones of the skull are identified on pages 28-29.)

NERVE HOLE
Many nerves lead to and from the brain through holes in the skull. This hole, the infra-orbital foramen, is for nerve branches from the upper incisor, canine and premolar teeth.

TOOTH HOLES
The bone of the jaw is spongy in texture and anchors the roots of the teeth.

NOSE HOLE
The protruding hump of the human nose is made of cartilage, not bone, so it is absent from the skeleton of the skull.

The teeth

An adult human has 32 teeth. In each jaw (upper and lower) there are four incisors at the front then, on each side, one canine, two premolars, and three molars. The enamel of a tooth is the hardest substance in the body.

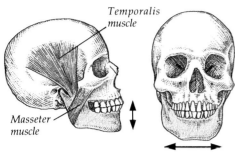

Temporalis muscle

Masseter muscle

ALL-AROUND CHEWING *above*
As we eat, the lower jaw moves up and down, and also from side to side, and even from front to back, for a really thorough chewing job. The tongue (which is almost all muscle) moves the food around the mouth; the cheek muscles keep food pressed between the teeth.

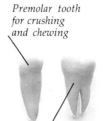

Incisor tooth for cutting and snipping

Premolar tooth for crushing and chewing

Canine tooth for piercing and tearing

Molar tooth for crushing and chewing

GROWING TEETH *right*
A young child has a set of 20 milk (deciduous) teeth. (Small jaws cannot hold more than that.) They fall out from the age of about six years, starting with those at the front.

INSIDE A TOOTH *right*
If a tooth is sliced open, various layers can be clearly seen inside. The outer layer is enamel, a hard, protective substance. Under this is a tough layer of dentine, which surrounds the pulp. Pulp contains nerves and blood vessels.

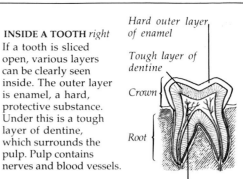

Hard outer layer of enamel

Tough layer of dentine

Crown

Root

Nerves and blood vessels of pulp

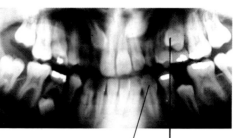

"Wraparound" x-ray of child's teeth

Milk tooth

Permanent tooth developing in gum

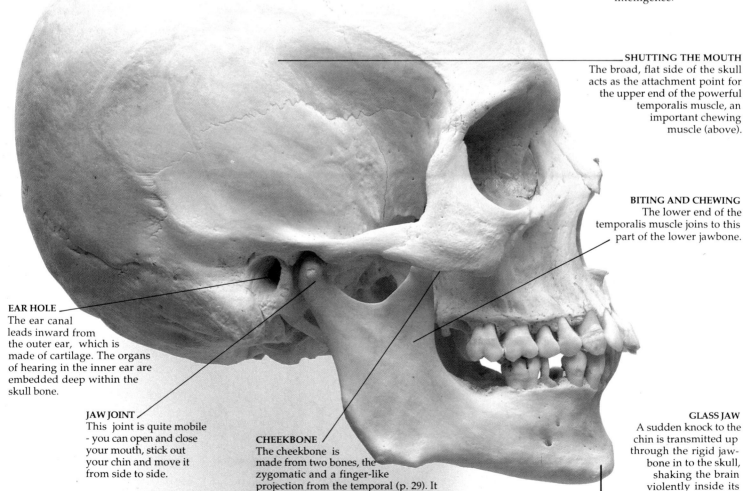

BRAIN DOME
The human forehead is more dome-shaped and bulging than that of our ape relatives. It houses the cerebral cortex - the part of the brain associated with intelligence.

SHUTTING THE MOUTH
The broad, flat side of the skull acts as the attachment point for the upper end of the powerful temporalis muscle, an important chewing muscle (above).

BITING AND CHEWING
The lower end of the temporalis muscle joins to this part of the lower jawbone.

EAR HOLE
The ear canal leads inward from the outer ear, which is made of cartilage. The organs of hearing in the inner ear are embedded deep within the skull bone.

JAW JOINT
This joint is quite mobile - you can open and close your mouth, stick out your chin and move it from side to side.

CHEEKBONE
The cheekbone is made from two bones, the zygomatic and a finger-like projection from the temporal (p. 29). It protects the lower eyeball and anchors the upper end of the masseter muscle, one of the main chewing muscles (above).

GLASS JAW
A sudden knock to the chin is transmitted up through the rigid jaw-bone in to the skull, shaking the brain violently inside its cushioning membranes (the meninges). This can result in unconsciousness - a knockout.

How the skull is built

THE HUMAN SKULL IN FACT starts life as an intricate curved jigsaw of nearly 30 separate pieces, sculpted in cartilage and membrane. During development these gradually turn to bone and grow together to form a solid case that protects the brain, eyes, inner ears, and other delicate sense organs. The separate bones are eventually knitted together with fibrous tissue. These joins, or "sutures", can be seen as wiggly lines on the skull. From the age of about 30 to 40 years, the sutures slowly fade and disappear. This is one way of telling the age of a skull's original owner. The cranium, or "braincase," is made of eight bones. There are 14 in the face, two in each side of the upper jaw, and one in each side of the lower jaw. The skull also encases the smallest bones in the body - the six tiny ossicles of the inner ears (p. 59).

A SKELETON PONDERS A SKULL
This engraving by the Belgian Vesalius (1514-64), the founding father of anatomy, is thought to have been Shakespeare's inspiration for the graveyard scene in *Hamlet*.

Two maxillae bear the top teeth and form the roof of the mouth

Inferior concha warms and moistens air as it enters the nose

The palatine bone makes up the back of the roof of the mouth

The lower back of the nasal cavity is called the vomer

The mandible, or lower jaw, consists of two firmly joined halves

The nasal bones make up the bridge of the nose

Inferior concha

Palatine bone

The fontaneles

During birth, the baby's head is squeezed as it passes along the birth canal (p. 45). Fontaneles are "soft spots" in the baby's skull, where the membrane has not yet turned to bone. They allow the skull bones to mold, slide, and even overlap, to minimize damage to the skull and brain. The largest of the six fontaneles is on the top of the skull. They disappear by one year of age.

Suture lines

Maxilla

Adult skull

Baby's skull

The pulsing of the baby's blood system can often be seen beneath the thin membrane layer of the uppermost fontanele.

The flattening face

Fossils found so far give us a broad outline of how the human skull may have evolved. Some of our probable ancestors are shown on the right. Gradually the face has become flatter, the teeth smaller, the chin less protruding, and the forehead more domed, to house the increasingly large brain.

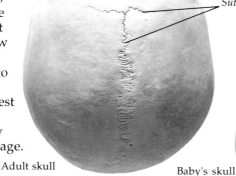

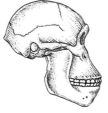
Australopithecus "Southern ape"

3-2 million years ago

Homo erectus "Upright man"

750,000 years ago

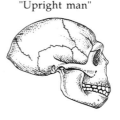
Homo sapiens neanderthalensis "Neanderthal man"

100,000-40,000 years ago

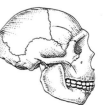

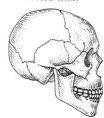
Homo sapiens sapiens "Wise man"

40,000 years ago to today

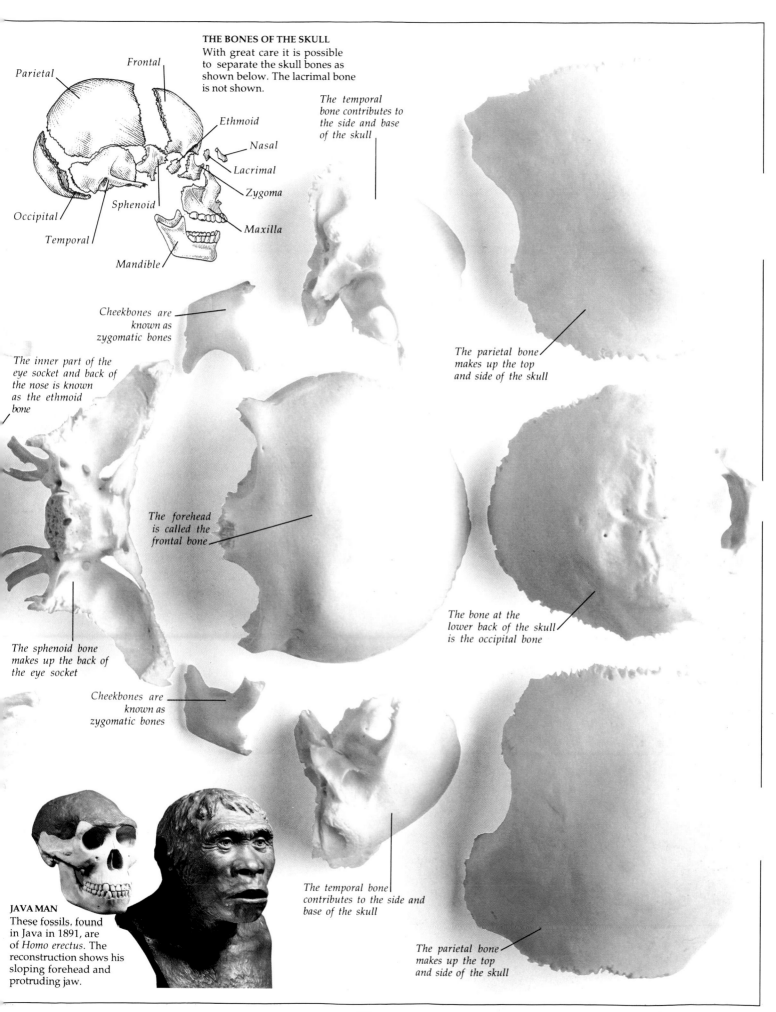

THE BONES OF THE SKULL
With great care it is possible to separate the skull bones as shown below. The lacrimal bone is not shown.

Parietal

Frontal

Ethmoid

Nasal

Lacrimal

Zygoma

Maxilla

Occipital

Sphenoid

Temporal

Mandible

The temporal bone contributes to the side and base of the skull

The parietal bone makes up the top and side of the skull

Cheekbones are known as zygomatic bones

The inner part of the eye socket and back of the nose is known as the ethmoid bone

The forehead is called the frontal bone

The bone at the lower back of the skull is the occipital bone

The sphenoid bone makes up the back of the eye socket

Cheekbones are known as zygomatic bones

The temporal bone contributes to the side and base of the skull

The parietal bone makes up the top and side of the skull

JAVA MAN
These fossils, found in Java in 1891, are of *Homo erectus*. The reconstruction shows his sloping forehead and protruding jaw.

Animal skulls

EACH SPECIES OF ANIMAL has a characteristic skull shape, molded by evolution to suit its particular way of life. Some skulls are light, with weight-saving gaps; others are thick and strong. Some are long and pointed, for probing and poking into holes; others are short and broad. All the skulls shown here have jaws: this may not seem very remarkable, but, in fact, jaws were a great step forward when they first evolved, in fish about 450 million years ago. They enabled their owners to catch large chunks of food and break it into pieces small enough to swallow. Before this, fish were jawless and restricted to sucking or sifting food from the mud.

GANNET
A powerful bird with a long, streamlined bill, the gannet dives from on high for fish.

AVOCET
Upturned bill for sifting sea water.

TAWNY OWL
Wide skull to house enormous eyes.

MERGANSER
This duck's notched bill grasps fish to eat.

AMAZON PARROT
A massive hooked bill shows its seed-cracking power.

BLACKBIRD
All-purpose bill for eating insects, worms, berries, and seeds.

CURLEW
Long bill probes for small creatures.

RABBIT
Its eyes are on the sides of its head, keeping an all-around watch for predators.

MALLARD
Wide, flattened bill "dabbles" in water for tiny bits of food.

HAMSTER
Gnaws at seeds and nuts with its large front teeth.

HEDGEHOG
Many, but similar, teeth indicate a diet of insects and other small animals.

FROG
Forward-facing eyes judge distance of prey for accurate hunting.

ARMADILLO
The long nose sniffs out ants and other small creatures.

THE LONG AND THE SHORT
In most kinds, or species, of animals, all individuals have a skull of much the same shape. All domestic dogs are one species, *Canis familiaris*. But over the centuries, people have selectively bred them for different features (below). Some have large, long skulls (usually working dogs) while smaller breeds tend to be more "decorative."

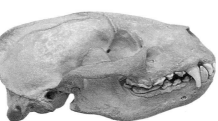

BADGER
Squat, heavy skull with long canine teeth point to a hunting way of life.

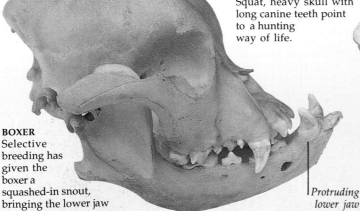

BOXER
Selective breeding has given the boxer a squashed-in snout, bringing the lower jaw to the front.

Protruding lower jaw

COLLIE
This breed has the more "natural" long muzzle of the dog's ancestor, the wolf.

Long muzzle

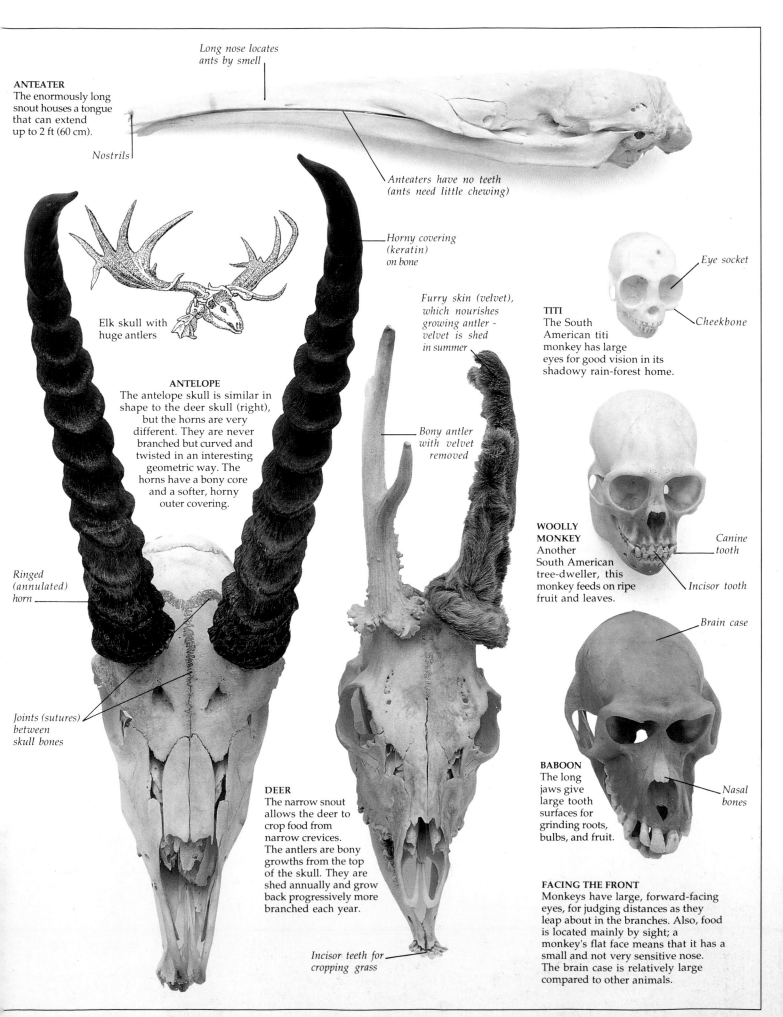

ANTEATER
The enormously long snout houses a tongue that can extend up to 2 ft (60 cm).

Long nose locates ants by smell

Nostrils

Anteaters have no teeth (ants need little chewing)

Elk skull with huge antlers

Horny covering (keratin) on bone

Furry skin (velvet), which nourishes growing antler - velvet is shed in summer

TITI
The South American titi monkey has large eyes for good vision in its shadowy rain-forest home.

Eye socket

Cheekbone

ANTELOPE
The antelope skull is similar in shape to the deer skull (right), but the horns are very different. They are never branched but curved and twisted in an interesting geometric way. The horns have a bony core and a softer, horny outer covering.

Bony antler with velvet removed

WOOLLY MONKEY
Another South American tree-dweller, this monkey feeds on ripe fruit and leaves.

Canine tooth

Incisor tooth

Ringed (annulated) horn

Brain case

Joints (sutures) between skull bones

DEER
The narrow snout allows the deer to crop food from narrow crevices. The antlers are bony growths from the top of the skull. They are shed annually and grow back progressively more branched each year.

BABOON
The long jaws give large tooth surfaces for grinding roots, bulbs, and fruit.

Nasal bones

Incisor teeth for cropping grass

FACING THE FRONT
Monkeys have large, forward-facing eyes, for judging distances as they leap about in the branches. Also, food is located mainly by sight; a monkey's flat face means that it has a small and not very sensitive nose. The brain case is relatively large compared to other animals.

Animal senses

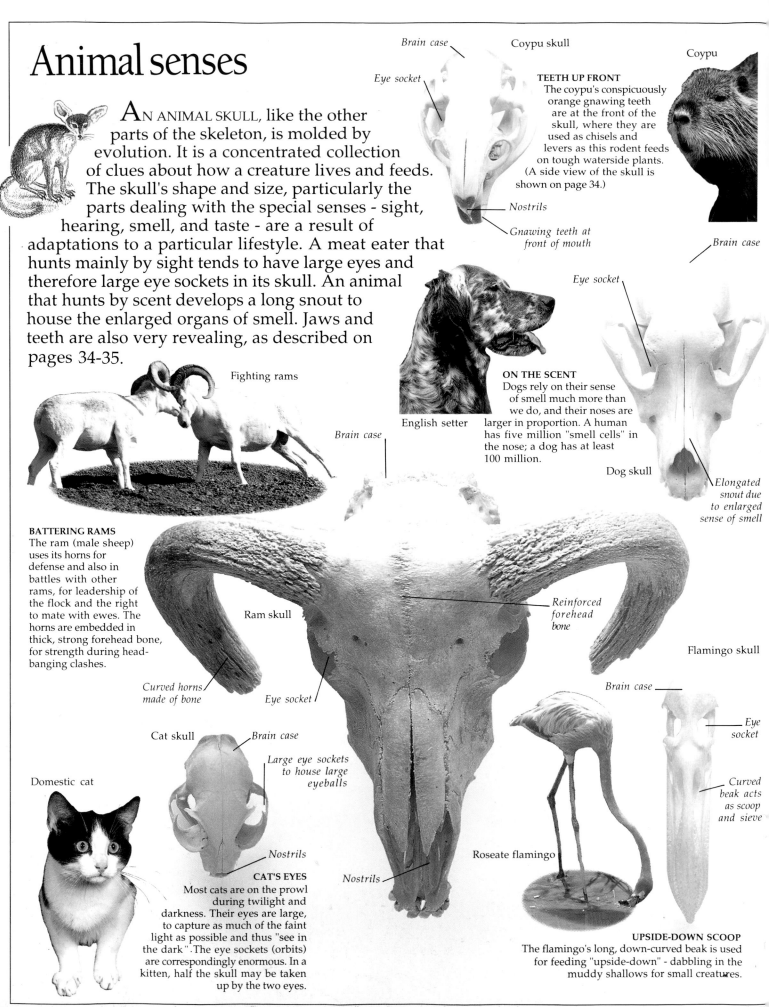

AN ANIMAL SKULL, like the other parts of the skeleton, is molded by evolution. It is a concentrated collection of clues about how a creature lives and feeds. The skull's shape and size, particularly the parts dealing with the special senses - sight, hearing, smell, and taste - are a result of adaptations to a particular lifestyle. A meat eater that hunts mainly by sight tends to have large eyes and therefore large eye sockets in its skull. An animal that hunts by scent develops a long snout to house the enlarged organs of smell. Jaws and teeth are also very revealing, as described on pages 34-35.

Brain case

Coypu skull

Eye socket

Coypu

TEETH UP FRONT
The coypu's conspicuously orange gnawing teeth are at the front of the skull, where they are used as chisels and levers as this rodent feeds on tough waterside plants. (A side view of the skull is shown on page 34.)

Nostrils

Gnawing teeth at front of mouth

Brain case

Eye socket

Fighting rams

English setter

Brain case

ON THE SCENT
Dogs rely on their sense of smell much more than we do, and their noses are larger in proportion. A human has five million "smell cells" in the nose; a dog has at least 100 million.

Dog skull

Elongated snout due to enlarged sense of smell

BATTERING RAMS
The ram (male sheep) uses its horns for defense and also in battles with other rams, for leadership of the flock and the right to mate with ewes. The horns are embedded in thick, strong forehead bone, for strength during head-banging clashes.

Ram skull

Reinforced forehead bone

Flamingo skull

Brain case

Curved horns made of bone

Eye socket

Cat skull

Brain case

Large eye sockets to house large eyeballs

Eye socket

Domestic cat

Nostrils

Curved beak acts as scoop and sieve

CAT'S EYES
Most cats are on the prowl during twilight and darkness. Their eyes are large, to capture as much of the faint light as possible and thus "see in the dark". The eye sockets (orbits) are correspondingly enormous. In a kitten, half the skull may be taken up by the two eyes.

Nostrils

Roseate flamingo

UPSIDE-DOWN SCOOP
The flamingo's long, down-curved beak is used for feeding "upside-down" - dabbling in the muddy shallows for small creatures.

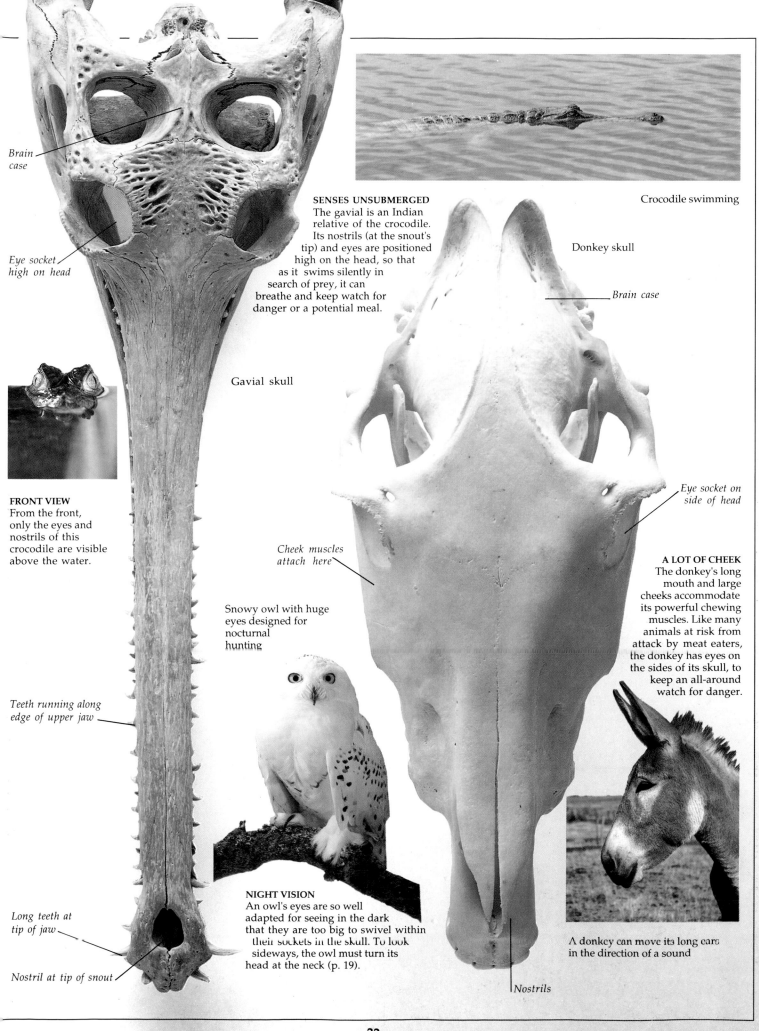

Brain
case

Eye socket
high on head

SENSES UNSUBMERGED
The gavial is an Indian
relative of the crocodile.
Its nostrils (at the snout's
tip) and eyes are positioned
high on the head, so that
as it swims silently in
search of prey, it can
breathe and keep watch for
danger or a potential meal.

Crocodile swimming

Donkey skull

Brain case

Gavial skull

Eye socket on
side of head

Cheek muscles
attach here

A LOT OF CHEEK
The donkey's long
mouth and large
cheeks accommodate
its powerful chewing
muscles. Like many
animals at risk from
attack by meat eaters,
the donkey has eyes on
the sides of its skull, to
keep an all-around
watch for danger.

FRONT VIEW
From the front,
only the eyes and
nostrils of this
crocodile are visible
above the water.

Snowy owl with huge
eyes designed for
nocturnal
hunting

Teeth running along
edge of upper jaw

Long teeth at
tip of jaw

NIGHT VISION
An owl's eyes are so well
adapted for seeing in the dark
that they are too big to swivel within
their sockets in the skull. To look
sideways, the owl must turn its
head at the neck (p. 19).

A donkey can move its long ears
in the direction of a sound

Nostril at tip of snout

Nostrils

33

Jaws and feeding

THE SHAPE OF AN animal's jaws and teeth tells us what type of food it eats. Long, thin jaws with small teeth toward the front are good at probing and nibbling. These jaws are useful for eating small items such as berries or insects. But such a design does not have the crushing power of short, broad jaws, with large teeth near the back. This type of jaw is useful for grinding tough plant material or cracking bone and gristle. Many animals have a combination design: medium-length jaws with sharp teeth at the front for cutting and snipping, and flat teeth at the back for crushing and grinding.

Rodents

Mice, rats, squirrels, and coypus are rodents. They are herbivores, but their front four teeth are large and sharp - specially adapted for gnawing.

Large areas to anchor jaw and neck muscles for biting and pulling

Coypu skull

Orange enamel on incisors

Gap for sealing mouth

Coypu

NON-STOP GNAWING
A rodent's front teeth never stop growing, but they are worn down continually by use. The gap in the tooth row allows the lips to seal off the inside of the mouth when gnawing.

Lower jaw moves up and down

Herbivores

Cows, horses, camels, sheep, goats, and deer are herbivores - they have a diet of plants. The lower jawbone is generally deep at the back, giving a large area to anchor the strong chewing muscle. Special jaw joints allow sideways movement of the jaws as well as up-and-down chewing.

Deep lower jaw for muscle attachment

Goat

Lower jaw moves from side to side and back and forth

Goat skull

Position of horny pad

Molar and premolar grinders

Gap allows tongue to manipulate bulky food

PULLING OFF A MOUTHFUL
Like many herbivores, the goat has no top front teeth. It pulls at food using its tough tongue and lips, its padded upper gums and small lower incisors (missing from this specimen). Its jaws also slide front-to-back for even better grinding.

Position of lower incisors

Omnivores

These are animals that eat both plant and animal foods - anything from small, soft berries to gristly chunks of meat. To cope with the varied diet, their jaws and teeth are usually less specialized than those of carnivores or herbivores.

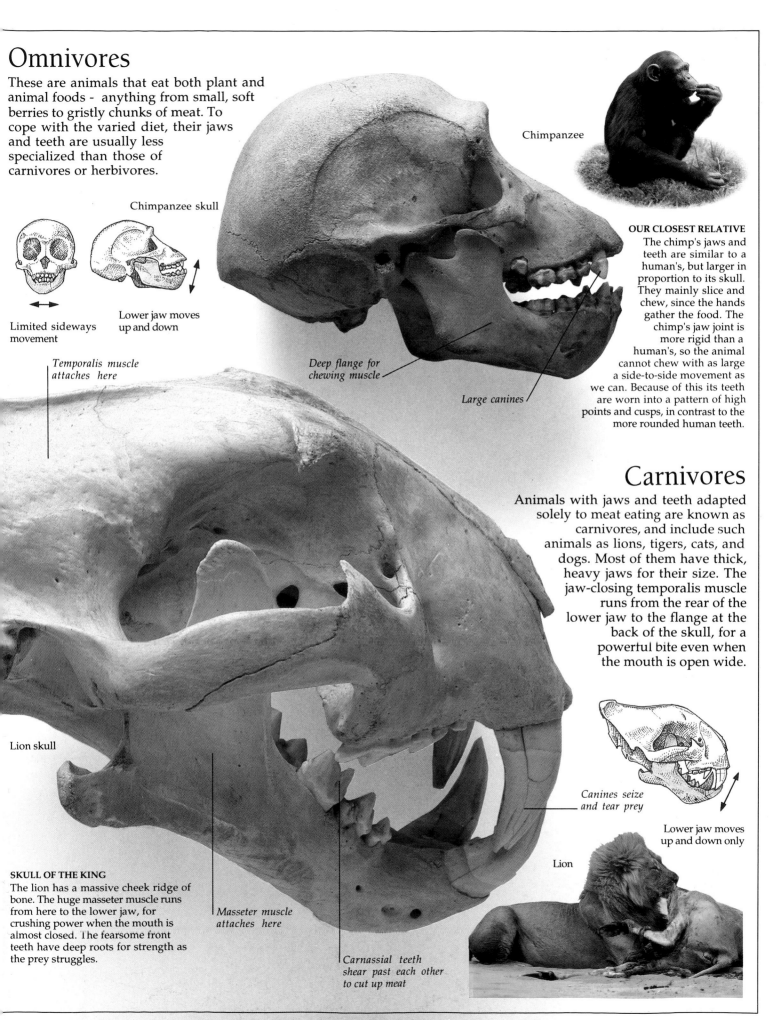

Chimpanzee

Chimpanzee skull

Limited sideways movement

Lower jaw moves up and down

Temporalis muscle attaches here

Deep flange for chewing muscle

Large canines

OUR CLOSEST RELATIVE
The chimp's jaws and teeth are similar to a human's, but larger in proportion to its skull. They mainly slice and chew, since the hands gather the food. The chimp's jaw joint is more rigid than a human's, so the animal cannot chew with as large a side-to-side movement as we can. Because of this its teeth are worn into a pattern of high points and cusps, in contrast to the more rounded human teeth.

Carnivores

Animals with jaws and teeth adapted solely to meat eating are known as carnivores, and include such animals as lions, tigers, cats, and dogs. Most of them have thick, heavy jaws for their size. The jaw-closing temporalis muscle runs from the rear of the lower jaw to the flange at the back of the skull, for a powerful bite even when the mouth is open wide.

Canines seize and tear prey

Lower jaw moves up and down only

Lion

Lion skull

SKULL OF THE KING
The lion has a massive cheek ridge of bone. The huge masseter muscle runs from here to the lower jaw, for crushing power when the mouth is almost closed. The fearsome front teeth have deep roots for strength as the prey struggles.

Masseter muscle attaches here

Carnassial teeth shear past each other to cut up meat

Animal teeth

BECAUSE OF THE NUMEROUS JOBS that animals' teeth are adapted to do, they vary widely in size and shape. Human teeth are relatively small and not particularly specialized we have cooking and knives and forks to help us. Animal teeth have to do many different jobs, from simple biting and slicing to chewing, crushing, and cracking, gnawing, grooming, digging, defending, and communicating. Teeth give many clues about their owner, from the type of food eaten to the age of the animal. The phrase "long in the tooth" refers to how the gums shrink in older animals and expose more of the tooth so it looks longer.

These leopards from Kenya were each made from the ivory of seven elephant tusks

The biggest teeth are elephant's tusks; the smallest, the teeth on a slug's tongue.

MOVING MOLARS
African elephant's molar tooth

Elephants have six molars on each side of the upper and lower jaws. These develop one by one and move forward in a conveyor-belt fashion. Only one or two teeth in each side of the jaw is in use at a time. When the last teeth have worn away, the animal can no longer eat. Ridges on the tooth improve its grinding efficiency.

Enamel ridge

Cement

Dentine between ridges

Rear root

Front root

IVORY HUNTERS *above*
Countless elephants died for their ivory tusks. Ivory was used for white piano keys, billiard balls, and exotic carvings. The killing is now controlled, but poaching continues.

Herbivores and carnivores

Herbivores, like horses and zebras (p. 34), must chew their food well before they swallow it, since unchewed plant material is difficult to digest chemically in the stomach and intestine. Their cheek teeth (molars) are broad and flat. Carnivores, animals that eat only meat (p. 35), have more pointed teeth for catching and slicing; less chewing is needed as meat is easier to digest.

Lower jawbone of horse

Incisors for grass cutting

Jawbone cut away to show long crowns

Dog's teeth

Molars

Broad surface for chewing

above **LONG-CROWNED MOLARS**
The horse's incisor teeth, at the front, grip and pull off mouthfuls of grass. The huge molars and premolars pulverize the food to a pulp. They are deeply anchored in the jaws, as can be seen above in the cutaway part of the horse's lower jawbone.

TEETH FOR TEARING AND SLICING
This selection of teeth from a dog's upper jaw shows carnivorous features. Each type of tooth has a special function and so assumes its particular shape.

Bone-cracking molar

Cutting carnassial

Crushing premolar

Long stabbing canine

Small gripping incisor

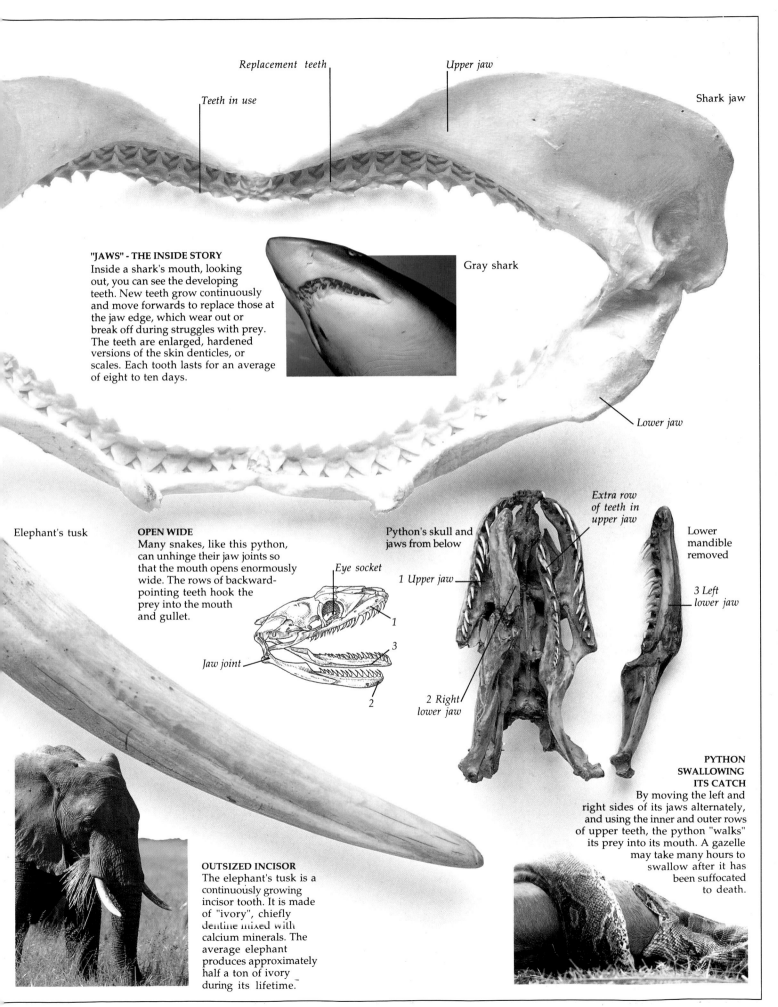

Replacement teeth

Teeth in use

Upper jaw

Shark jaw

"JAWS" - THE INSIDE STORY
Inside a shark's mouth, looking out, you can see the developing teeth. New teeth grow continuously and move forwards to replace those at the jaw edge, which wear out or break off during struggles with prey. The teeth are enlarged, hardened versions of the skin denticles, or scales. Each tooth lasts for an average of eight to ten days.

Gray shark

Lower jaw

Elephant's tusk

OPEN WIDE
Many snakes, like this python, can unhinge their jaw joints so that the mouth opens enormously wide. The rows of backward-pointing teeth hook the prey into the mouth and gullet.

Eye socket

Jaw joint

1

3

2

Python's skull and jaws from below

Extra row of teeth in upper jaw

1 Upper jaw

2 Right lower jaw

Lower mandible removed

3 Left lower jaw

PYTHON SWALLOWING ITS CATCH
By moving the left and right sides of its jaws alternately, and using the inner and outer rows of upper teeth, the python "walks" its prey into its mouth. A gazelle may take many hours to swallow after it has been suffocated to death.

OUTSIZED INCISOR
The elephant's tusk is a continuously growing incisor tooth. It is made of "ivory", chiefly dentine mixed with calcium minerals. The average elephant produces approximately half a ton of ivory during its lifetime.

The human spine

THE SPINE is literally the "back bone" of the human body. It forms a vertical supporting rod for the head, arms, and legs. It allows us to stoop and squat, to turn and nod the head, and to twist the shoulders and hips. Yet it was originally designed as a horizontal girder, to take the weight of the chest and abdomen: the original prehistoric mammals almost certainly moved on all fours (p. 46). In the upright human, the spine has an S-shaped curve when seen from the side, to balance the various parts of the body over the legs and feet and reduce muscle strain when standing. The human spine works on the chain-link principle: many small movements add up. Each vertebra can only move a little in relation to its neighbors. But over the whole row this means the back can bend double. The spine shown below is "lying on its side", with the head end to the left and the "tail" on the right.

This engraving, from an anatomy book of 1685, features a back view of the human skeleton

THE CURVED SPINE *above*
From the side, the spine has a slight S-shape. This helps to bring the centers of gravity of the head, arms, chest and abdomen above the legs, so that the body as a whole is well balanced.

BELOW THE SKULL
The first two vertebrae are called the atlas and the axis. All of the upper spine contributes to head movements, but these top two vertebrae are specialized to allow the head to nod and twist.

Atlas allows nodding movements

Axis allows side to side movements

IN THE NECK
There are seven vertebrae in the neck, called the cervical vertebrae. They allow us to turn our head in roughly three-quarters of a circle without moving the shoulders. (By moving our eyes as well, we can see in a complete circle.) Muscles run from the "wings" (transverse processes and neural spine) on the sides and rear of each vertebra to the skull, shoulder blades, and lower vertebrae. This steadies the head on the neck.

Cervical vertebra from behind

IN THE CHEST
The vertebrae become larger the lower they are in the spine, since they have to carry increasing weight. There are 12 chest (or thoracic) vertebrae, one for each pair of ribs. The ribs join to shallow cups on the body of the vertebra. The upper 10 pairs of ribs also join to hollows on the transverse processes for extra stability. These two sets of joints move slightly every time you breathe.

Thoracic vertebra from behind

Shallow socket for end of rib

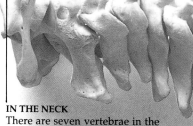

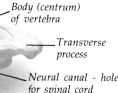

A NOD AND A SHAKE
The topmost vertebra, the atlas, allows nodding movements of the head. Side to side movements are a result of the atlas swiveling on the axis.

Cervical vertebra from top

Body (centrum) of vertebra

Transverse process

Neural canal - hole for spinal cord

Neural arch

Neural spine

Thoracic vertebra from top

Transverse process

Neural spine

The protective role of the spine

The large holes in each vertebra line up to form a bony tunnel or canal. Inside this, well protected from knocks and twists, is the delicate spinal cord. Nerves enter and leave the cord through gaps between neighboring vertebrae. Occasionally, a disc of cartilage between two vertebrae is squashed and presses on the nerve, causing the pain of a "slipped disc."

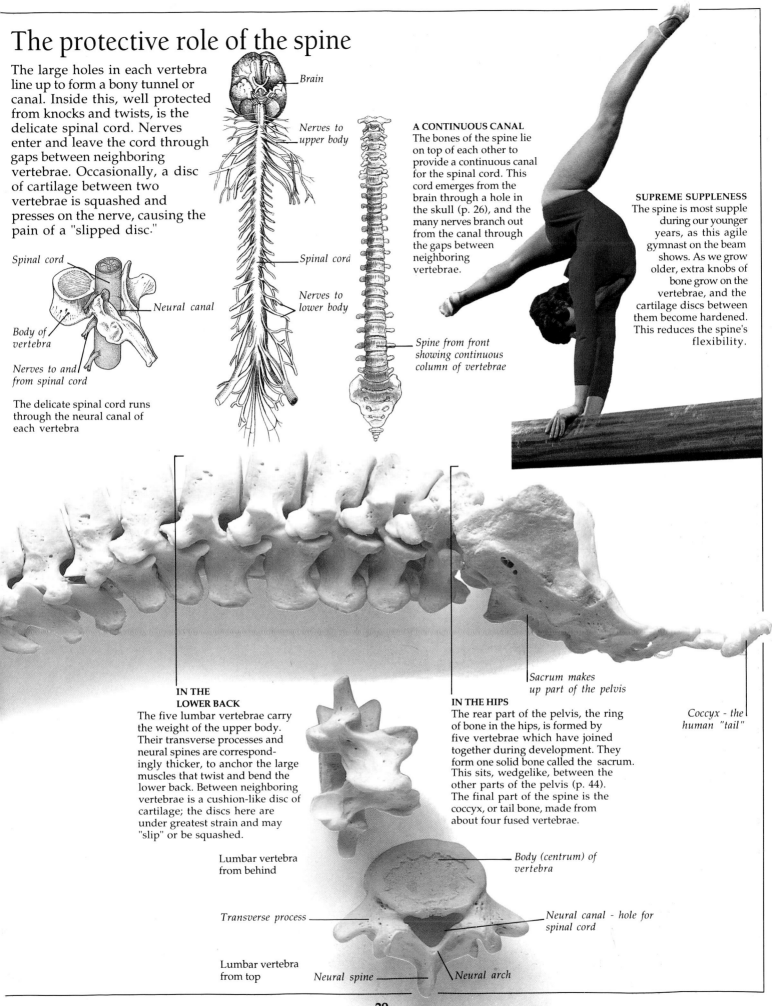

Brain

Nerves to upper body

Spinal cord

Nerves to lower body

Spinal cord

Neural canal

Body of vertebra

Nerves to and from spinal cord

The delicate spinal cord runs through the neural canal of each vertebra

A CONTINUOUS CANAL
The bones of the spine lie on top of each other to provide a continuous canal for the spinal cord. This cord emerges from the brain through a hole in the skull (p. 26), and the many nerves branch out from the canal through the gaps between neighboring vertebrae.

Spine from front showing continuous column of vertebrae

SUPREME SUPPLENESS
The spine is most supple during our younger years, as this agile gymnast on the beam shows. As we grow older, extra knobs of bone grow on the vertebrae, and the cartilage discs between them become hardened. This reduces the spine's flexibility.

IN THE LOWER BACK
The five lumbar vertebrae carry the weight of the upper body. Their transverse processes and neural spines are correspondingly thicker, to anchor the large muscles that twist and bend the lower back. Between neighboring vertebrae is a cushion-like disc of cartilage; the discs here are under greatest strain and may "slip" or be squashed.

Lumbar vertebra from behind

IN THE HIPS
The rear part of the pelvis, the ring of bone in the hips, is formed by five vertebrae which have joined together during development. They form one solid bone called the sacrum. This sits, wedgelike, between the other parts of the pelvis (p. 44). The final part of the spine is the coccyx, or tail bone, made from about four fused vertebrae.

Sacrum makes up part of the pelvis

Coccyx - the human "tail"

Body (centrum) of vertebra

Neural canal - hole for spinal cord

Transverse process

Lumbar vertebra from top

Neural spine

Neural arch

Animal backbones

EVERY FISH, REPTILE, amphibian, bird, and mammal has a row of bones in its back, usually called the spine or spinal column. This is the feature that groups them together as vertebrates (animals with backbones or vertebrae), distinguishing them from invertebrates such as insects and worms (p. 22). The basic spine design is a row of small bones, linked together into a flexible column, with the skull at one end and a tail (usually) at the other. However, the number of individual vertebrae varies from as few as nine in a frog to more than 400 in some snakes!

A GRIPPING TAIL
The end of the lemur's spine - its tail - is prehensile and serves as a fifth limb, to grip branches while climbing. This also leaves both hands free when feeding.

Ring-tailed lemurs

Nose to tail length - 35 in (89 cm)

First two vertebrae allow head to twist and nod

HEAD TO TAIL
A fox has about 50 vertebrae; about half of these are in its "brush" or tail. Those in the hip region have large flanges (ridges) for the muscles and ligaments that secure the pelvis.

Red fox

Region of stomach

SLITHERING ALONG
In a snake each vertebra, with its pair of ribs, is virtually identical to all the others. A snake's skeleton is all backbone as it has no arms, legs, shoulder blades, or pelvis. Large snakes, such as this python, use their belly scales to move. The scales, attached to the ribs, are pushed backwards in groups; their rear edges are tilted down to grip the ground.

Shoulder blades linked here

Python skeleton

Reticulated python

Skull

Region of heart

Lower jaw

AGILE REPTILES
Lack of limbs does not seem to restrict snakes, such as this reticulated python. They can move very fast, climb, swim, and burrow.

Rib

Region of intestine

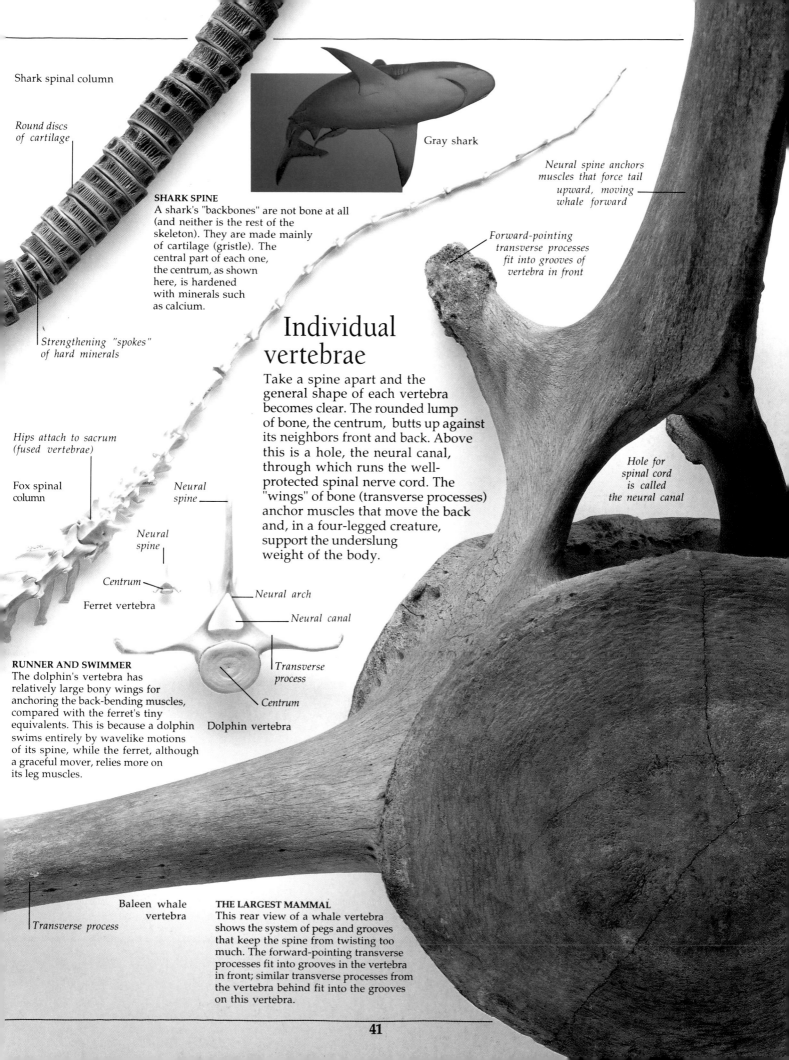

Shark spinal column

Round discs of cartilage

SHARK SPINE
A shark's "backbones" are not bone at all (and neither is the rest of the skeleton). They are made mainly of cartilage (gristle). The central part of each one, the centrum, as shown here, is hardened with minerals such as calcium.

Gray shark

Strengthening "spokes" of hard minerals

Neural spine anchors muscles that force tail upward, moving whale forward

Forward-pointing transverse processes fit into grooves of vertebra in front

Individual vertebrae

Take a spine apart and the general shape of each vertebra becomes clear. The rounded lump of bone, the centrum, butts up against its neighbors front and back. Above this is a hole, the neural canal, through which runs the well-protected spinal nerve cord. The "wings" of bone (transverse processes) anchor muscles that move the back and, in a four-legged creature, support the underslung weight of the body.

Hips attach to sacrum (fused vertebrae)

Fox spinal column

Neural spine

Hole for spinal cord is called the neural canal

Neural spine

Centrum

Ferret vertebra

Neural arch

Neural canal

Transverse process

Centrum

RUNNER AND SWIMMER
The dolphin's vertebra has relatively large bony wings for anchoring the back-bending muscles, compared with the ferret's tiny equivalents. This is because a dolphin swims entirely by wavelike motions of its spine, while the ferret, although a graceful mover, relies more on its leg muscles.

Dolphin vertebra

Baleen whale vertebra

Transverse process

THE LARGEST MAMMAL
This rear view of a whale vertebra shows the system of pegs and grooves that keep the spine from twisting too much. The forward-pointing transverse processes fit into grooves in the vertebra in front; similar transverse processes from the vertebra behind fit into the grooves on this vertebra.

The rib cage

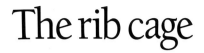

PROBLEM: the lungs need to inflate and deflate, becoming larger and smaller as they breathe; yet they also need protection against being knocked or crushed. A solid case of protective bone, like the skull around the brain, would be too rigid. Answer: a flexible cage with movable bars - the ribs. Closely spaced, with tough ligaments and muscles between them, the ribs give good protection to the delicate lungs. In addition, each rib is thin and flexible, so that it can absorb knocks without cracking and puncturing the vital airtight seal around the lungs. The ribs move at the points where they join the spine and breastbone. When breathing in, muscles lift the ribs upwards and swing them outward, increasing the volume of the chest and sucking air into the lungs.

Inside the chest

The ribs protect the lungs and also the other organs in the chest, such as the heart and main blood vessels. And they guard the stomach, liver, and other parts of the upper abdomen. These organs nestle under the diaphragm, a dome-shaped muscle that forms the base of the chest, so they are above the level of the bottom ribs.

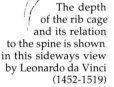

The depth of the rib cage and its relation to the spine is shown in this sideways view by Leonardo da Vinci (1452-1519)

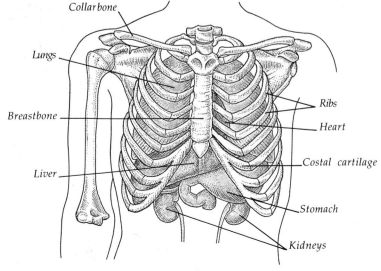

Collarbone

Breastbone

A CAGE OF BONY BARS
The chest cage is made up of the spine at the back, 12 pairs of ribs arched around the sides, and the breastbone in front.

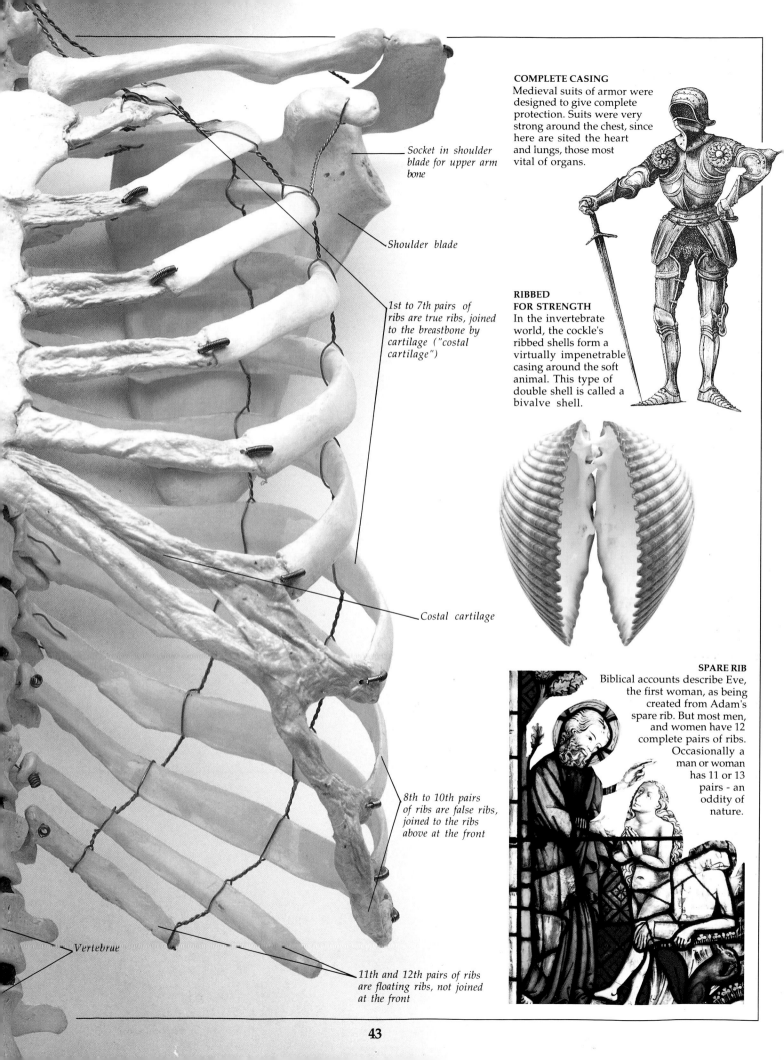

Socket in shoulder blade for upper arm bone

Shoulder blade

1st to 7th pairs of ribs are true ribs, joined to the breastbone by cartilage ("costal cartilage")

Costal cartilage

8th to 10th pairs of ribs are false ribs, joined to the ribs above at the front

Vertebrae

11th and 12th pairs of ribs are floating ribs, not joined at the front

COMPLETE CASING
Medieval suits of armor were designed to give complete protection. Suits were very strong around the chest, since here are sited the heart and lungs, those most vital of organs.

RIBBED
FOR STRENGTH
In the invertebrate world, the cockle's ribbed shells form a virtually impenetrable casing around the soft animal. This type of double shell is called a bivalve shell.

SPARE RIB
Biblical accounts describe Eve, the first woman, as being created from Adam's spare rib. But most men, and women have 12 complete pairs of ribs. Occasionally a man or woman has 11 or 13 pairs - an oddity of nature.

Human hip bones

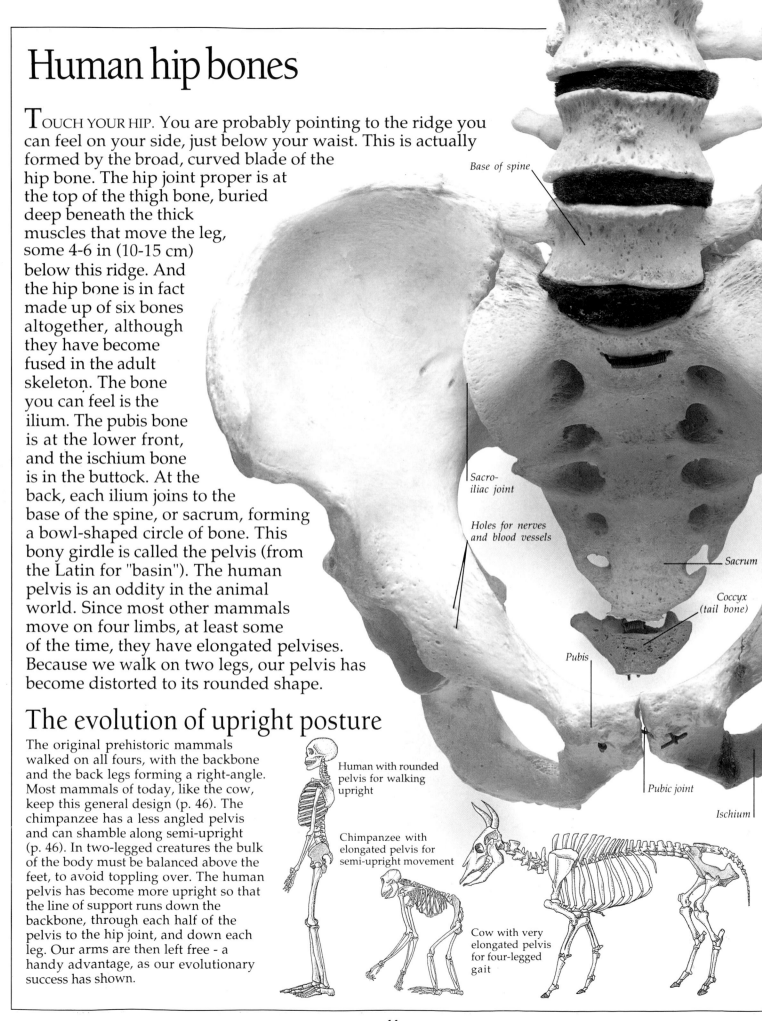

Touch your hip. You are probably pointing to the ridge you can feel on your side, just below your waist. This is actually formed by the broad, curved blade of the hip bone. The hip joint proper is at the top of the thigh bone, buried deep beneath the thick muscles that move the leg, some 4-6 in (10-15 cm) below this ridge. And the hip bone is in fact made up of six bones altogether, although they have become fused in the adult skeleton. The bone you can feel is the ilium. The pubis bone is at the lower front, and the ischium bone is in the buttock. At the back, each ilium joins to the base of the spine, or sacrum, forming a bowl-shaped circle of bone. This bony girdle is called the pelvis (from the Latin for "basin"). The human pelvis is an oddity in the animal world. Since most other mammals move on four limbs, at least some of the time, they have elongated pelvises. Because we walk on two legs, our pelvis has become distorted to its rounded shape.

The evolution of upright posture

The original prehistoric mammals walked on all fours, with the backbone and the back legs forming a right-angle. Most mammals of today, like the cow, keep this general design (p. 46). The chimpanzee has a less angled pelvis and can shamble along semi-upright (p. 46). In two-legged creatures the bulk of the body must be balanced above the feet, to avoid toppling over. The human pelvis has become more upright so that the line of support runs down the backbone, through each half of the pelvis to the hip joint, and down each leg. Our arms are then left free - a handy advantage, as our evolutionary success has shown.

Base of spine

Sacro-iliac joint

Holes for nerves and blood vessels

Sacrum

Coccyx (tail bone)

Pubis

Pubic joint

Ischium

Human with rounded pelvis for walking upright

Chimpanzee with elongated pelvis for semi-upright movement

Cow with very elongated pelvis for four-legged gait

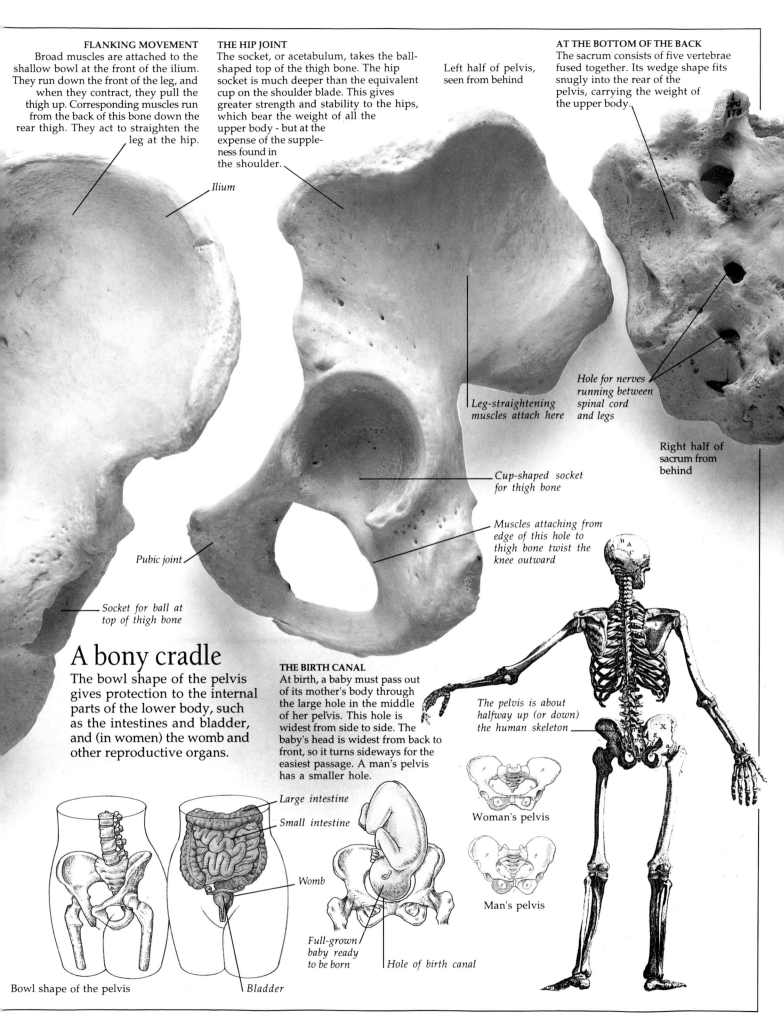

FLANKING MOVEMENT
Broad muscles are attached to the shallow bowl at the front of the ilium. They run down the front of the leg, and when they contract, they pull the thigh up. Corresponding muscles run from the back of this bone down the rear thigh. They act to straighten the leg at the hip.

Ilium

THE HIP JOINT
The socket, or acetabulum, takes the ball-shaped top of the thigh bone. The hip socket is much deeper than the equivalent cup on the shoulder blade. This gives greater strength and stability to the hips, which bear the weight of all the upper body - but at the expense of the suppleness found in the shoulder.

Left half of pelvis, seen from behind

AT THE BOTTOM OF THE BACK
The sacrum consists of five vertebrae fused together. Its wedge shape fits snugly into the rear of the pelvis, carrying the weight of the upper body.

Leg-straightening muscles attach here

Hole for nerves running between spinal cord and legs

Right half of sacrum from behind

Cup-shaped socket for thigh bone

Pubic joint

Muscles attaching from edge of this hole to thigh bone twist the knee outward

Socket for ball at top of thigh bone

A bony cradle
The bowl shape of the pelvis gives protection to the internal parts of the lower body, such as the intestines and bladder, and (in women) the womb and other reproductive organs.

THE BIRTH CANAL
At birth, a baby must pass out of its mother's body through the large hole in the middle of her pelvis. This hole is widest from side to side. The baby's head is widest from back to front, so it turns sideways for the easiest passage. A man's pelvis has a smaller hole.

The pelvis is about halfway up (or down) the human skeleton

Large intestine

Small intestine

Womb

Full-grown baby ready to be born

Hole of birth canal

Woman's pelvis

Man's pelvis

Bowl shape of the pelvis

Bladder

Animal hip bones

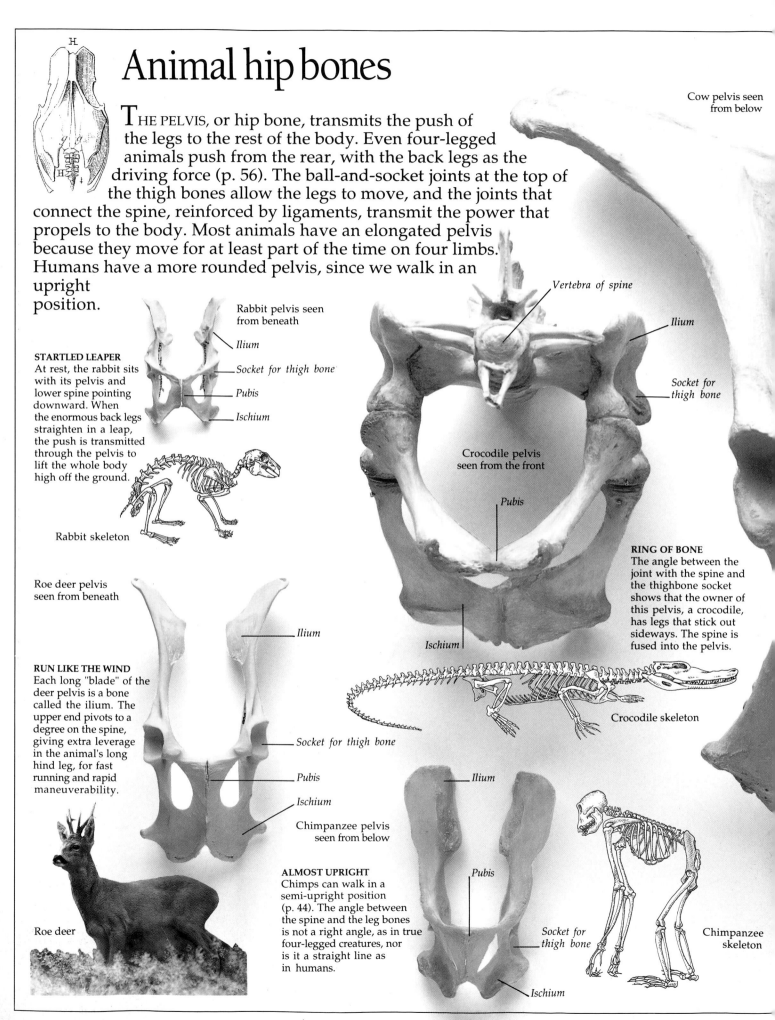

THE PELVIS, or hip bone, transmits the push of the legs to the rest of the body. Even four-legged animals push from the rear, with the back legs as the driving force (p. 56). The ball-and-socket joints at the top of the thigh bones allow the legs to move, and the joints that connect the spine, reinforced by ligaments, transmit the power that propels to the body. Most animals have an elongated pelvis because they move for at least part of the time on four limbs. Humans have a more rounded pelvis, since we walk in an upright position.

Cow pelvis seen from below

STARTLED LEAPER
At rest, the rabbit sits with its pelvis and lower spine pointing downward. When the enormous back legs straighten in a leap, the push is transmitted through the pelvis to lift the whole body high off the ground.

Rabbit pelvis seen from beneath

Ilium

Socket for thigh bone

Pubis

Ischium

Rabbit skeleton

Roe deer pelvis seen from beneath

RUN LIKE THE WIND
Each long "blade" of the deer pelvis is a bone called the ilium. The upper end pivots to a degree on the spine, giving extra leverage in the animal's long hind leg, for fast running and rapid maneuverability.

Ilium

Socket for thigh bone

Pubis

Ischium

Roe deer

Vertebra of spine

Ilium

Socket for thigh bone

Crocodile pelvis seen from the front

Pubis

Ischium

RING OF BONE
The angle between the joint with the spine and the thighbone socket shows that the owner of this pelvis, a crocodile, has legs that stick out sideways. The spine is fused into the pelvis.

Crocodile skeleton

Chimpanzee pelvis seen from below

ALMOST UPRIGHT
Chimps can walk in a semi-upright position (p. 44). The angle between the spine and the leg bones is not a right angle, as in true four-legged creatures, nor is it a straight line as in humans.

Ilium

Pubis

Socket for thigh bone

Ischium

Chimpanzee skeleton

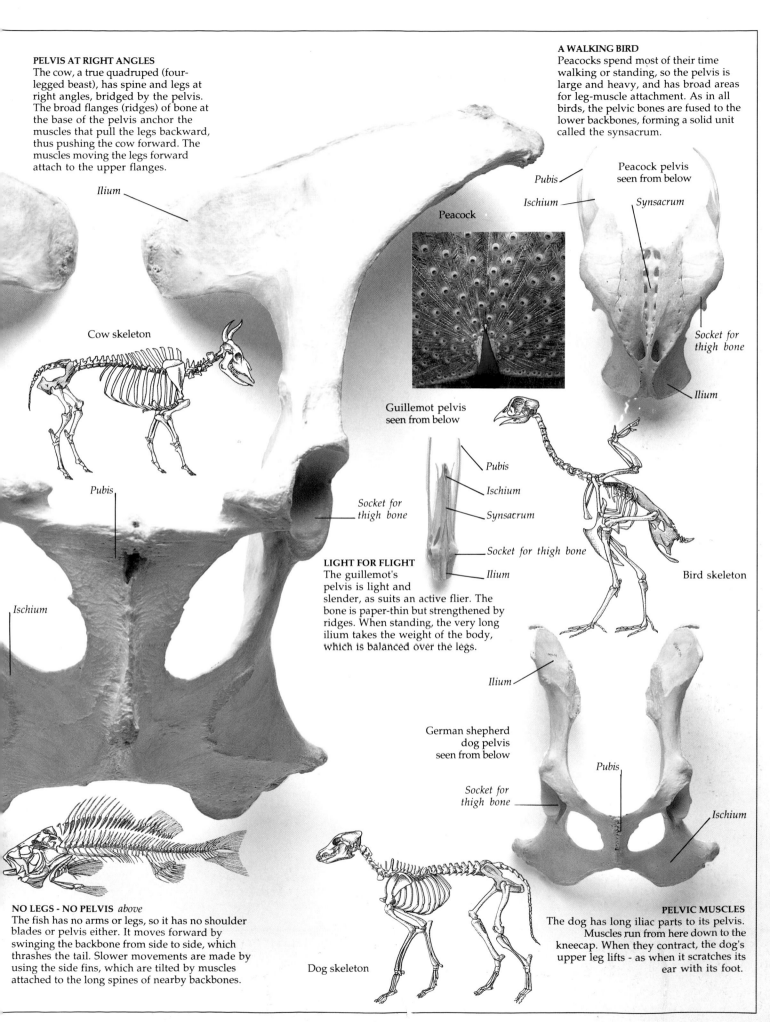

PELVIS AT RIGHT ANGLES
The cow, a true quadruped (four-legged beast), has spine and legs at right angles, bridged by the pelvis. The broad flanges (ridges) of bone at the base of the pelvis anchor the muscles that pull the legs backward, thus pushing the cow forward. The muscles moving the legs forward attach to the upper flanges.

Ilium

Cow skeleton

Pubis

Ischium

A WALKING BIRD
Peacocks spend most of their time walking or standing, so the pelvis is large and heavy, and has broad areas for leg-muscle attachment. As in all birds, the pelvic bones are fused to the lower backbones, forming a solid unit called the synsacrum.

Pubis

Peacock pelvis seen from below

Ischium

Synsacrum

Peacock

Socket for thigh bone

Ilium

Guillemot pelvis seen from below

Socket for thigh bone

Pubis

Ischium

Synsacrum

Socket for thigh bone

Ilium

LIGHT FOR FLIGHT
The guillemot's pelvis is light and slender, as suits an active flier. The bone is paper-thin but strengthened by ridges. When standing, the very long ilium takes the weight of the body, which is balanced over the legs.

Bird skeleton

Ilium

German shepherd dog pelvis seen from below

Socket for thigh bone

Pubis

Ischium

NO LEGS - NO PELVIS *above*
The fish has no arms or legs, so it has no shoulder blades or pelvis either. It moves forward by swinging the backbone from side to side, which thrashes the tail. Slower movements are made by using the side fins, which are tilted by muscles attached to the long spines of nearby backbones.

Dog skeleton

PELVIC MUSCLES
The dog has long iliac parts to its pelvis. Muscles run from here down to the kneecap. When they contract, the dog's upper leg lifts - as when it scratches its ear with its foot.

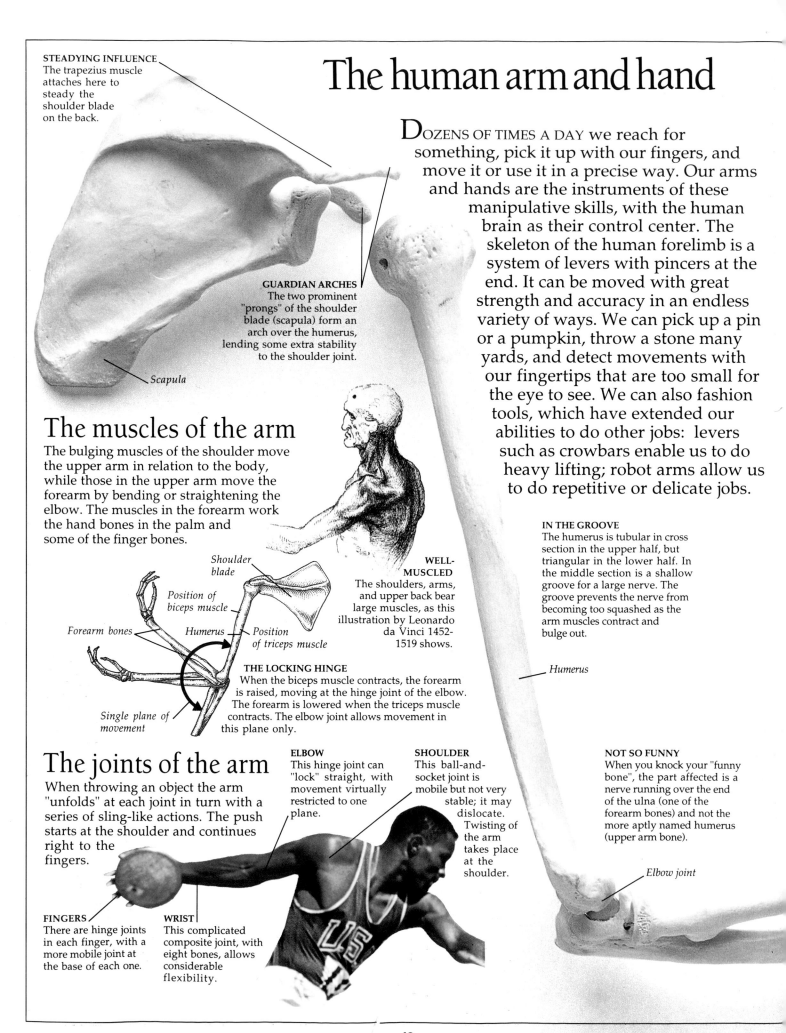

STEADYING INFLUENCE
The trapezius muscle attaches here to steady the shoulder blade on the back.

GUARDIAN ARCHES
The two prominent "prongs" of the shoulder blade (scapula) form an arch over the humerus, lending some extra stability to the shoulder joint.

Scapula

DOZENS OF TIMES A DAY we reach for something, pick it up with our fingers, and move it or use it in a precise way. Our arms and hands are the instruments of these manipulative skills, with the human brain as their control center. The skeleton of the human forelimb is a system of levers with pincers at the end. It can be moved with great strength and accuracy in an endless variety of ways. We can pick up a pin or a pumpkin, throw a stone many yards, and detect movements with our fingertips that are too small for the eye to see. We can also fashion tools, which have extended our abilities to do other jobs: levers such as crowbars enable us to do heavy lifting; robot arms allow us to do repetitive or delicate jobs.

The muscles of the arm

The bulging muscles of the shoulder move the upper arm in relation to the body, while those in the upper arm move the forearm by bending or straightening the elbow. The muscles in the forearm work the hand bones in the palm and some of the finger bones.

Shoulder blade

Position of biceps muscle

Forearm bones

Humerus

Position of triceps muscle

Single plane of movement

WELL-MUSCLED
The shoulders, arms, and upper back bear large muscles, as this illustration by Leonardo da Vinci 1452-1519 shows.

THE LOCKING HINGE
When the biceps muscle contracts, the forearm is raised, moving at the hinge joint of the elbow. The forearm is lowered when the triceps muscle contracts. The elbow joint allows movement in this plane only.

IN THE GROOVE
The humerus is tubular in cross section in the upper half, but triangular in the lower half. In the middle section is a shallow groove for a large nerve. The groove prevents the nerve from becoming too squashed as the arm muscles contract and bulge out.

Humerus

The joints of the arm

When throwing an object the arm "unfolds" at each joint in turn with a series of sling-like actions. The push starts at the shoulder and continues right to the fingers.

ELBOW
This hinge joint can "lock" straight, with movement virtually restricted to one plane.

SHOULDER
This ball-and-socket joint is mobile but not very stable; it may dislocate. Twisting of the arm takes place at the shoulder.

NOT SO FUNNY
When you knock your "funny bone", the part affected is a nerve running over the end of the ulna (one of the forearm bones) and not the more aptly named humerus (upper arm bone).

Elbow joint

FINGERS
There are hinge joints in each finger, with a more mobile joint at the base of each one.

WRIST
This complicated composite joint, with eight bones, allows considerable flexibility.

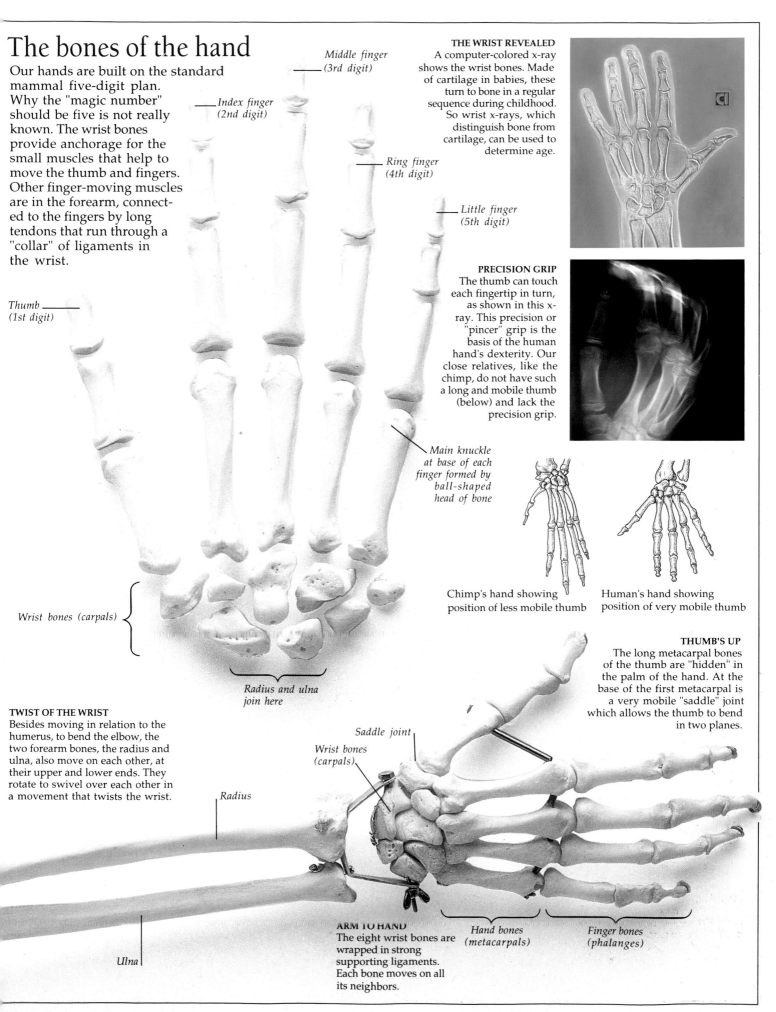

The bones of the hand

Our hands are built on the standard mammal five-digit plan. Why the "magic number" should be five is not really known. The wrist bones provide anchorage for the small muscles that help to move the thumb and fingers. Other finger-moving muscles are in the forearm, connected to the fingers by long tendons that run through a "collar" of ligaments in the wrist.

Thumb
(1st digit)

Middle finger
(3rd digit)

Index finger
(2nd digit)

Ring finger
(4th digit)

Little finger
(5th digit)

Wrist bones (carpals)

Radius and ulna join here

THE WRIST REVEALED
A computer-colored x-ray shows the wrist bones. Made of cartilage in babies, these turn to bone in a regular sequence during childhood. So wrist x-rays, which distinguish bone from cartilage, can be used to determine age.

PRECISION GRIP
The thumb can touch each fingertip in turn, as shown in this x-ray. This precision or "pincer" grip is the basis of the human hand's dexterity. Our close relatives, like the chimp, do not have such a long and mobile thumb (below) and lack the precision grip.

Main knuckle at base of each finger formed by ball-shaped head of bone

Chimp's hand showing position of less mobile thumb

Human's hand showing position of very mobile thumb

THUMB'S UP
The long metacarpal bones of the thumb are "hidden" in the palm of the hand. At the base of the first metacarpal is a very mobile "saddle" joint which allows the thumb to bend in two planes.

TWIST OF THE WRIST
Besides moving in relation to the humerus, to bend the elbow, the two forearm bones, the radius and ulna, also move on each other, at their upper and lower ends. They rotate to swivel over each other in a movement that twists the wrist.

Radius

Ulna

Saddle joint

Wrist bones (carpals)

ARM TO HAND
The eight wrist bones are wrapped in strong supporting ligaments. Each bone moves on all its neighbors.

Hand bones (metacarpals)

Finger bones (phalanges)

Arms, wings, and flippers

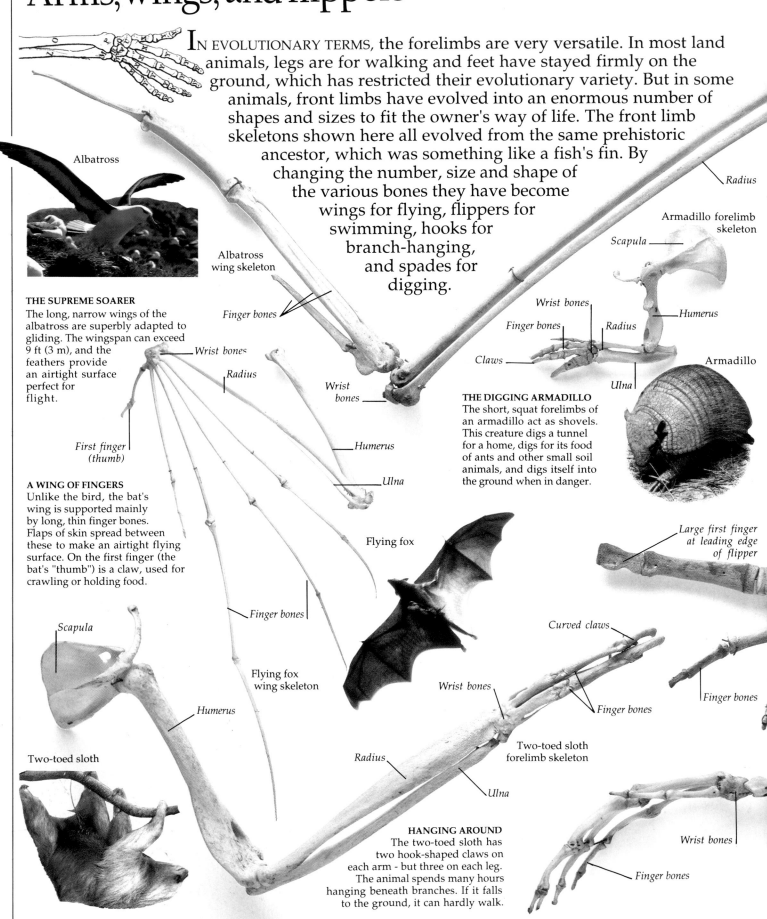

IN EVOLUTIONARY TERMS, the forelimbs are very versatile. In most land animals, legs are for walking and feet have stayed firmly on the ground, which has restricted their evolutionary variety. But in some animals, front limbs have evolved into an enormous number of shapes and sizes to fit the owner's way of life. The front limb skeletons shown here all evolved from the same prehistoric ancestor, which was something like a fish's fin. By changing the number, size and shape of the various bones they have become wings for flying, flippers for swimming, hooks for branch-hanging, and spades for digging.

Albatross

Albatross wing skeleton

THE SUPREME SOARER
The long, narrow wings of the albatross are superbly adapted to gliding. The wingspan can exceed 9 ft (3 m), and the feathers provide an airtight surface perfect for flight.

Finger bones

Wrist bones

Radius

First finger (thumb)

Wrist bones

A WING OF FINGERS
Unlike the bird, the bat's wing is supported mainly by long, thin finger bones. Flaps of skin spread between these to make an airtight flying surface. On the first finger (the bat's "thumb") is a claw, used for crawling or holding food.

Humerus

Ulna

Scapula

Humerus

Finger bones

Two-toed sloth

Flying fox

Flying fox wing skeleton

Radius

Armadillo forelimb skeleton

Scapula

Wrist bones

Finger bones

Radius

Humerus

Claws

Ulna

Armadillo

THE DIGGING ARMADILLO
The short, squat forelimbs of an armadillo act as shovels. This creature digs a tunnel for a home, digs for its food of ants and other small soil animals, and digs itself into the ground when in danger.

Large first finger at leading edge of flipper

Curved claws

Wrist bones

Finger bones

Finger bones

Two-toed sloth forelimb skeleton

Radius

Ulna

HANGING AROUND
The two-toed sloth has two hook-shaped claws on each arm - but three on each leg. The animal spends many hours hanging beneath branches. If it falls to the ground, it can hardly walk.

Wrist bones

Finger bones

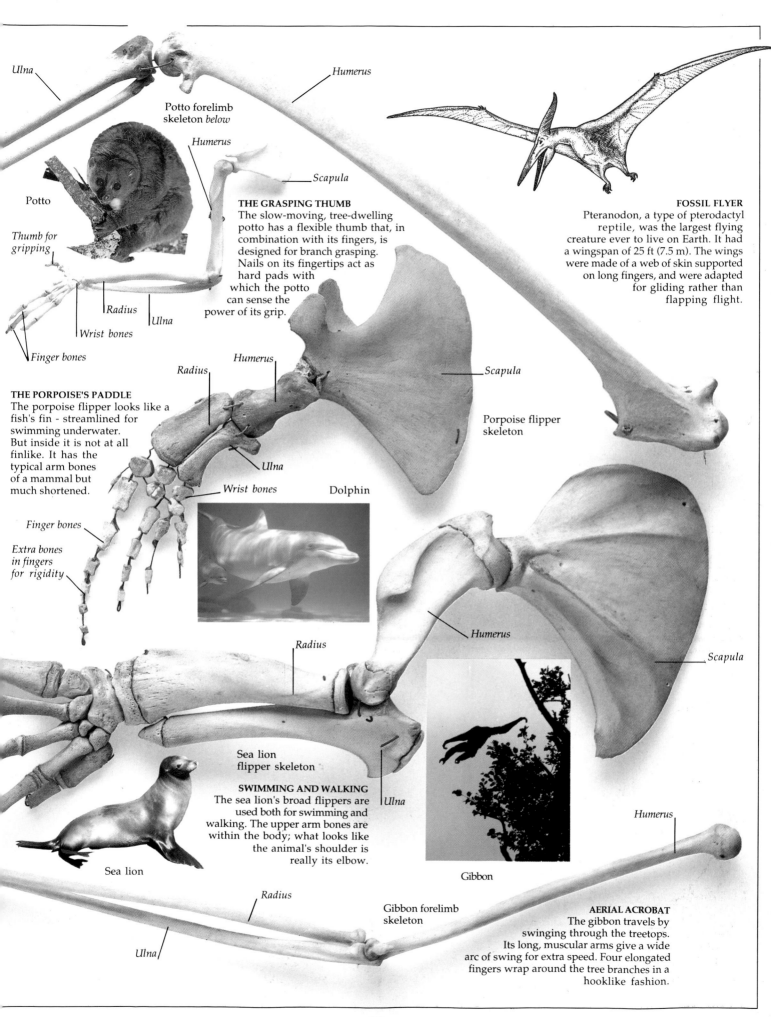

Ulna

Humerus

Potto forelimb skeleton *below*

Humerus

Potto

Scapula

Thumb for gripping

THE GRASPING THUMB
The slow-moving, tree-dwelling potto has a flexible thumb that, in combination with its fingers, is designed for branch grasping. Nails on its fingertips act as hard pads with which the potto can sense the power of its grip.

FOSSIL FLYER
Pteranodon, a type of pterodactyl reptile, was the largest flying creature ever to live on Earth. It had a wingspan of 25 ft (7.5 m). The wings were made of a web of skin supported on long fingers, and were adapted for gliding rather than flapping flight.

Radius

Ulna

Wrist bones

Finger bones

Humerus

Radius

Scapula

Ulna

Porpoise flipper skeleton

THE PORPOISE'S PADDLE
The porpoise flipper looks like a fish's fin - streamlined for swimming underwater. But inside it is not at all finlike. It has the typical arm bones of a mammal but much shortened.

Wrist bones

Dolphin

Finger bones

Extra bones in fingers for rigidity

Humerus

Scapula

Radius

Sea lion flipper skeleton

SWIMMING AND WALKING
The sea lion's broad flippers are used both for swimming and walking. The upper arm bones are within the body; what looks like the animal's shoulder is really its elbow.

Ulna

Humerus

Sea lion

Gibbon

Radius

Gibbon forelimb skeleton

AERIAL ACROBAT
The gibbon travels by swinging through the treetops. Its long, muscular arms give a wide arc of swing for extra speed. Four elongated fingers wrap around the tree branches in a hooklike fashion.

Ulna

Animal shoulder blades

FROM THE OUTSIDE, the four limbs of a four-legged animal look much the same. But inside, the skeleton reveals many differences. The back legs are designed mainly for moving the whole body forward when walking, running, or jumping (p. 56). The front legs, on the other hand, do various jobs. They cushion the body when landing after a leap; they may move and hold food or objects; and they can strike at prey or enemies. So they need to be more flexible. The key to their wider range of movement is the shoulder blade, or scapula. This triangle of bone connects to the body chiefly by muscles that run to the backbone and ribs, and which can tilt the scapula at many angles. And it links to the forelimb by a ball-and-socket joint, giving even greater flexibility.

Red fox

Red fox shoulder blade

ON THE TROT
The fox's broad shoulder blade has a large surface area for muscle anchorage, indicating that it moves for much of the time on all fours. Foxes may also dig for food with their front legs.

Collared peccary shoulder blade

STIFF-LEGGED PIG
The long, narrow shoulder blade of the collared peccary, a type of pig, is swung forward and back by the muscles connecting it to the body. The legs are relatively short and thin, resulting in a rather stiff-legged walk.

Pig skeleton

Beaver holding twig it is gnawing

DAM BUILDER
The beaver's smallish shoulder blade shows that its short front limbs are not weight carriers. They are manipulators for holding food and prodding twigs and mud into dams.

Beaver shoulder blade

Wallaby shoulder blade

CROUCHING TO DRINK
A Siberian tiger lowers itself over a pool to drink. Its spine is lowered between its front legs, and the shoulder blades show clearly on each side of the body.

TWO-LEGGED HOPPING
The forelimbs of a kangaroo or wallaby take no part in its fast hopping movements. They are used to fight and play, to pick up food, and to lean on when grazing.

Kangaroo skeleton

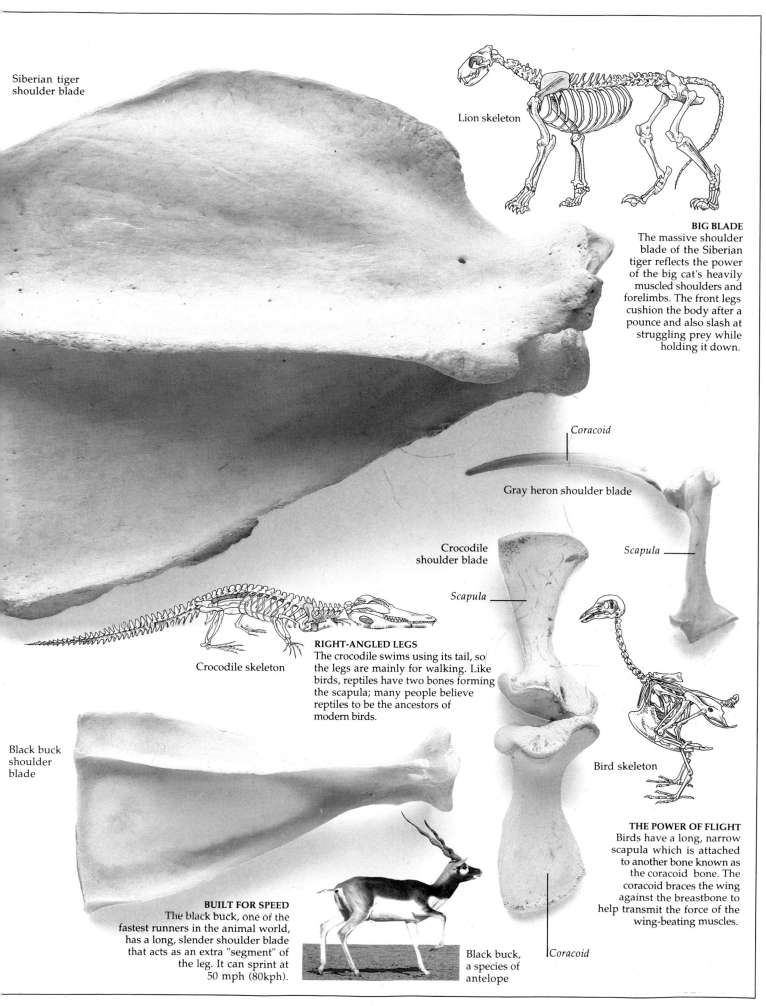

Siberian tiger
shoulder blade

Lion skeleton

BIG BLADE
The massive shoulder
blade of the Siberian
tiger reflects the power
of the big cat's heavily
muscled shoulders and
forelimbs. The front legs
cushion the body after a
pounce and also slash at
struggling prey while
holding it down.

Coracoid

Gray heron shoulder blade

Scapula

Crocodile
shoulder blade

Scapula

RIGHT-ANGLED LEGS
The crocodile swims using its tail, so
the legs are mainly for walking. Like
birds, reptiles have two bones forming
the scapula; many people believe
reptiles to be the ancestors of
modern birds.

Crocodile skeleton

Bird skeleton

Black buck
shoulder
blade

THE POWER OF FLIGHT
Birds have a long, narrow
scapula which is attached
to another bone known as
the coracoid bone. The
coracoid braces the wing
against the breastbone to
help transmit the force of the
wing-beating muscles.

BUILT FOR SPEED
The black buck, one of the
fastest runners in the animal world,
has a long, slender shoulder blade
that acts as an extra "segment" of
the leg. It can sprint at
50 mph (80kph).

Black buck,
a species of
antelope

Coracoid

The human leg and foot

WE ARE SO used to standing and watching the world go by that we are not usually aware of what an amazing balancing feat this is. Other animals may be able to stand on their back limbs temporarily, but they usually topple over after a few seconds. We can maintain a fully upright, two-legged posture for hours, leaving our arms and hands free for other tasks. Compared to the arm (p. 48), the bones of the human leg are thick and strong, to carry the body's weight. We do not walk on our toes, like many creatures (p. 56). Our feet are broad and also long, for good stability, and our toes are much smaller than in most other animals. Small muscle adjustments take place continuously in the neck, arms, back, and legs, keeping our weight over our feet. Walking requires the coordination and contraction of dozens of muscles. It has been called "controlled falling": the body tilts forwards, so that it begins to tip over, only to be saved from falling by moving a foot forward.

Head of thigh bone

THE HEAD OF THE LEG
The thigh bone is the largest single bone in the body. At its top end, or "head", it is reinforced by ridges that anchor powerful leg-moving muscles.

LONG, YET STRONG
In accordance with good engineering design, the shaft of the thigh bone is long and tubelike. It is subjected to fewer stresses and strains along its length than at the ends.

SWINGING ARMS
As you walk, the arm on one side swings forward as the leg on that side swings back. The two movements partly cancel each other out, keeping the body's weight mostly in the center.

The muscles and joints of the leg

The muscles at the hip, thigh, and calf move the limbs at the joints. Those at the hip swing the leg forward and backward at the hip joint, as when walking. The muscles at the back of the thigh bend the knee at its hinge joint. Those in the calf straighten the foot at the ankle joint.

THE HIP
This ball-and-socket joint combines great strength with some mobility. The ball of the thigh bone is at an angle to the shaft so as to come more directly under the middle of the body.

THE KNEE
This joint works like a hinge, its main movements being forward and backward. It cannot cope with too much twisting, which might dislocate it.

THE ANKLE
Seven bones make up the ankle, a composite joint. Each bone moves a little in relation to its neighbors, giving great overall strength with limited flexibility.

MUSCLES FOR MOVING THE LEG
This rear view of the legs shows all the muscles important in movement.

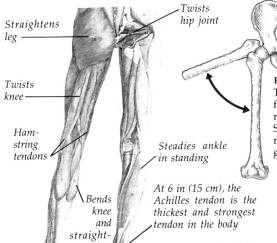

Straightens leg

Twists knee

Ham-string tendons

Bends knee and straightens foot

Twists hip joint

Steadies ankle in standing

At 6 in (15 cm), the Achilles tendon is the thickest and strongest tendon in the body

Twists sole of foot inwards

HIP LIMITS
The hip moves easily from front to back for running and walking. Side-to-side movement is limited but good for suddenly changing direction.

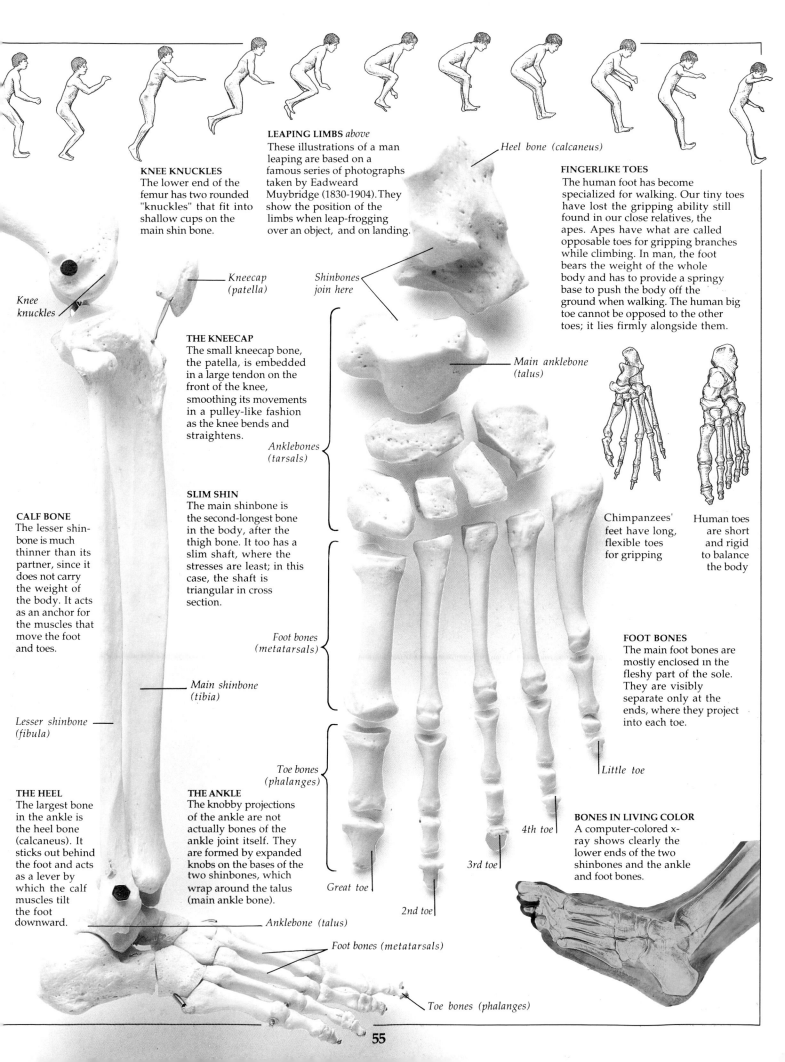

KNEE KNUCKLES
The lower end of the femur has two rounded "knuckles" that fit into shallow cups on the main shin bone.

Knee knuckles

Knee knuckles

Kneecap (patella)

LEAPING LIMBS *above*
These illustrations of a man leaping are based on a famous series of photographs taken by Eadweard Muybridge (1830-1904). They show the position of the limbs when leap-frogging over an object, and on landing.

Heel bone (calcaneus)

Shinbones join here

FINGERLIKE TOES
The human foot has become specialized for walking. Our tiny toes have lost the gripping ability still found in our close relatives, the apes. Apes have what are called opposable toes for gripping branches while climbing. In man, the foot bears the weight of the whole body and has to provide a springy base to push the body off the ground when walking. The human big toe cannot be opposed to the other toes; it lies firmly alongside them.

THE KNEECAP
The small kneecap bone, the patella, is embedded in a large tendon on the front of the knee, smoothing its movements in a pulley-like fashion as the knee bends and straightens.

Main anklebone (talus)

Anklebones (tarsals)

SLIM SHIN
The main shinbone is the second-longest bone in the body, after the thigh bone. It too has a slim shaft, where the stresses are least; in this case, the shaft is triangular in cross section.

Chimpanzees' feet have long, flexible toes for gripping

Human toes are short and rigid to balance the body

CALF BONE
The lesser shin-bone is much thinner than its partner, since it does not carry the weight of the body. It acts as an anchor for the muscles that move the foot and toes.

Foot bones (metatarsals)

FOOT BONES
The main foot bones are mostly enclosed in the fleshy part of the sole. They are visibly separate only at the ends, where they project into each toe.

Main shinbone (tibia)

Lesser shinbone (fibula)

Toe bones (phalanges)

Little toe

4th toe

THE HEEL
The largest bone in the ankle is the heel bone (calcaneus). It sticks out behind the foot and acts as a lever by which the calf muscles tilt the foot downward.

THE ANKLE
The knobby projections of the ankle are not actually bones of the ankle joint itself. They are formed by expanded knobs on the bases of the two shinbones, which wrap around the talus (main ankle bone).

Great toe

3rd toe

2nd toe

BONES IN LIVING COLOR
A computer-colored x-ray shows clearly the lower ends of the two shinbones and the ankle and foot bones.

Anklebone (talus)

Foot bones (metatarsals)

Toe bones (phalanges)

55

Animal legs

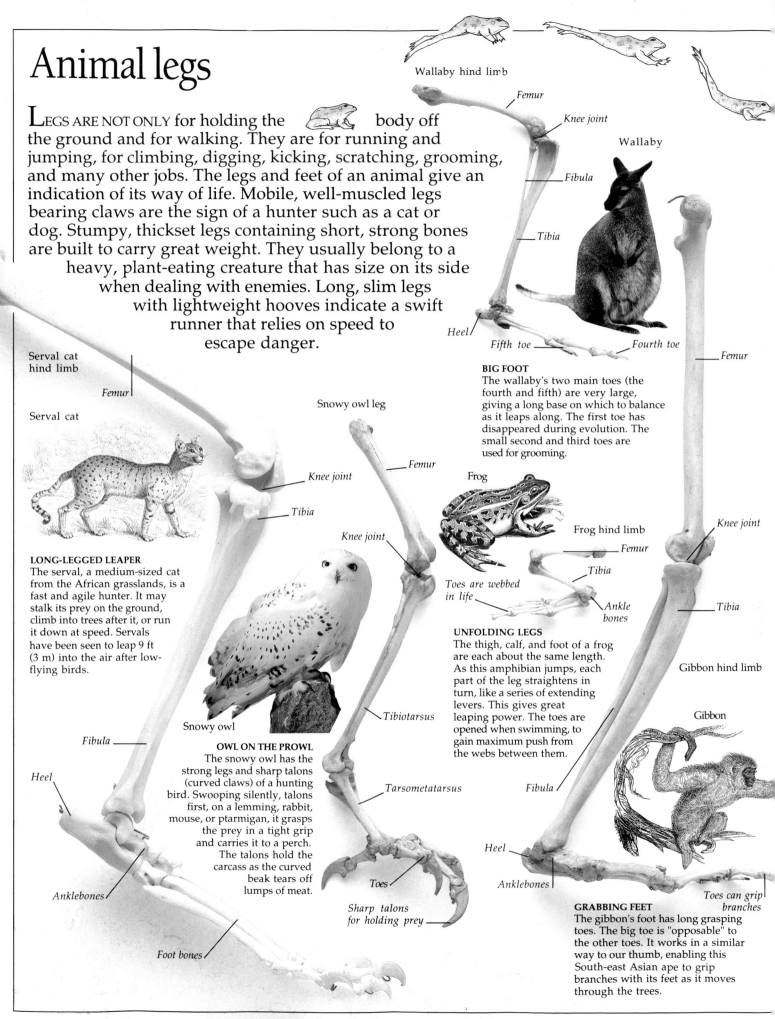

LEGS ARE NOT ONLY for holding the body off the ground and for walking. They are for running and jumping, for climbing, digging, kicking, scratching, grooming, and many other jobs. The legs and feet of an animal give an indication of its way of life. Mobile, well-muscled legs bearing claws are the sign of a hunter such as a cat or dog. Stumpy, thickset legs containing short, strong bones are built to carry great weight. They usually belong to a heavy, plant-eating creature that has size on its side when dealing with enemies. Long, slim legs with lightweight hooves indicate a swift runner that relies on speed to escape danger.

Wallaby hind limb

Femur

Knee joint

Wallaby

Fibula

Tibia

Heel

Fifth toe

Fourth toe

BIG FOOT
The wallaby's two main toes (the fourth and fifth) are very large, giving a long base on which to balance as it leaps along. The first toe has disappeared during evolution. The small second and third toes are used for grooming.

Femur

Serval cat hind limb

Femur

Serval cat

Snowy owl leg

Frog

Femur

Knee joint

Frog hind limb

Femur

Knee joint

Tibia

Knee joint

Tibia

LONG-LEGGED LEAPER
The serval, a medium-sized cat from the African grasslands, is a fast and agile hunter. It may stalk its prey on the ground, climb into trees after it, or run it down at speed. Servals have been seen to leap 9 ft (3 m) into the air after low-flying birds.

Knee joint

Tibia

Toes are webbed in life

Ankle bones

Gibbon hind limb

Gibbon

UNFOLDING LEGS
The thigh, calf, and foot of a frog are each about the same length. As this amphibian jumps, each part of the leg straightens in turn, like a series of extending levers. This gives great leaping power. The toes are opened when swimming, to gain maximum push from the webs between them.

Fibula

Heel

Tibiotarsus

Snowy owl

OWL ON THE PROWL
The snowy owl has the strong legs and sharp talons (curved claws) of a hunting bird. Swooping silently, talons first, on a lemming, rabbit, mouse, or ptarmigan, it grasps the prey in a tight grip and carries it to a perch. The talons hold the carcass as the curved beak tears off lumps of meat.

Fibula

Tarsometatarsus

Fibula

Heel

Anklebones

Toes

Sharp talons for holding prey

Heel

Anklebones

Toes can grip branches

GRABBING FEET
The gibbon's foot has long grasping toes. The big toe is "opposable" to the other toes. It works in a similar way to our thumb, enabling this South-east Asian ape to grip branches with its feet as it moves through the trees.

Foot bones

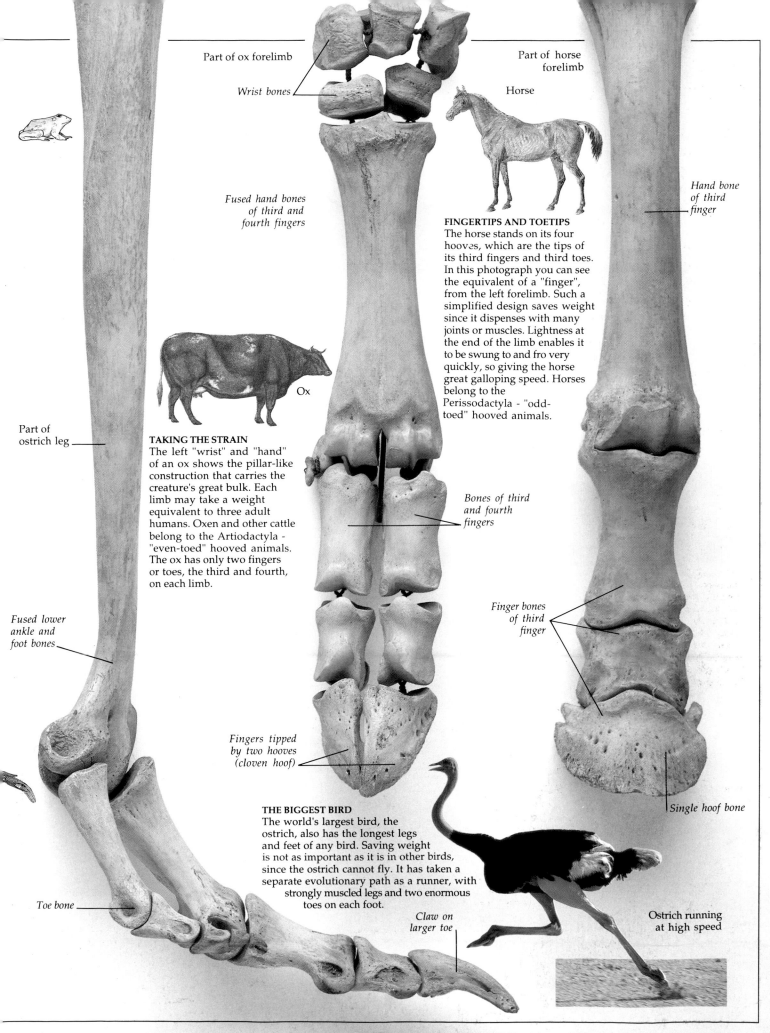

Part of ox forelimb

Part of horse forelimb

Wrist bones

Horse

Fused hand bones of third and fourth fingers

Hand bone of third finger

FINGERTIPS AND TOETIPS
The horse stands on its four hooves, which are the tips of its third fingers and third toes. In this photograph you can see the equivalent of a "finger", from the left forelimb. Such a simplified design saves weight since it dispenses with many joints or muscles. Lightness at the end of the limb enables it to be swung to and fro very quickly, so giving the horse great galloping speed. Horses belong to the Perissodactyla - "odd-toed" hooved animals.

Part of ostrich leg

Ox

TAKING THE STRAIN
The left "wrist" and "hand" of an ox shows the pillar-like construction that carries the creature's great bulk. Each limb may take a weight equivalent to three adult humans. Oxen and other cattle belong to the Artiodactyla - "even-toed" hooved animals. The ox has only two fingers or toes, the third and fourth, on each limb.

Bones of third and fourth fingers

Fused lower ankle and foot bones

Finger bones of third finger

Fingers tipped by two hooves (cloven hoof)

Single hoof bone

THE BIGGEST BIRD
The world's largest bird, the ostrich, also has the longest legs and feet of any bird. Saving weight is not as important as it is in other birds, since the ostrich cannot fly. It has taken a separate evolutionary path as a runner, with strongly muscled legs and two enormous toes on each foot.

Toe bone

Claw on larger toe

Ostrich running at high speed

The largest and smallest bones

BONES, LIKE OTHER PARTS OF THE BODY, vary in exact size and shape from person to person. Tall people have longer bones than shorter people, especially in the legs, where the thigh bone makes up about one-quarter of the body's height. Most of these variations in bone length are slight, however, with the average man being taller than the average woman. Occasionally a disease or inherited condition affects development of bones as the baby grows in the womb. Or bone growth during childhood, which is controlled mainly by hormones, may be affected by disease, illness, or a poor diet. The result is an unusually tall or small person.

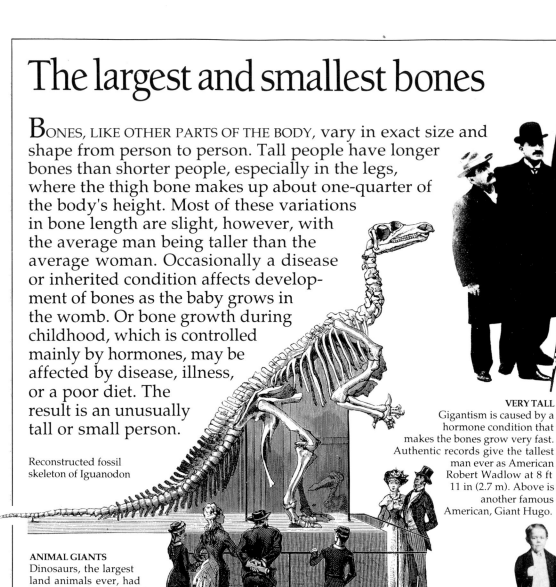

Reconstructed fossil skeleton of Iguanodon

Giant Hugo

ANIMAL GIANTS
Dinosaurs, the largest land animals ever, had gigantic bones. The thigh bone of this Iguanodon (p. 12) was 4 ft 3 in (1.3 m) long. Some dinosaur arm bones were nearly 9 ft (3 m) long!

VERY TALL
Gigantism is caused by a hormone condition that makes the bones grow very fast. Authentic records give the tallest man ever as American Robert Wadlow at 8 ft 11 in (2.7 m). Above is another famous American, Giant Hugo.

VERY SMALL
The smallest humans measure about 2 ft to 2 ft 6 in (60 cm to 75 cm). One of the best-known midgets, shown here with his midget wife, was Charles Stratton ("General Tom Thumb") who was 3 ft 4 in (1.02 m) short.

"Tom Thumb" at his wedding

The size of the thighs

This array of 10 thigh bones (femurs) shows the enormous size differences within the mammal group. In general, fast-moving animals have long, slender leg bones in relation to their body size. The seal's femurs are a special case: they are within the body, and this animal swims using its back flippers, which contain its shin and feet bones.

RABBIT
Body length - 12 in (30 cm)
Femur length - 3 in (8 cm)

HEDGEHOG
Body length - 8 in (20 cm)
Femur length - 1.6 in (4 cm)

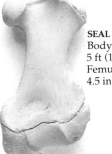

SEAL
Body length - 5 ft (1.6 m)
Femur length - 4.5 in (11 cm)

DOG (BASSET HOUND)
Body length - 2 ft 4 in (70 cm)
Femur length - 4.5 in (11 cm)

CAT left
Body length - 1 ft 8 in (50 cm)
Femur length - 5 in (12 cm)

SHEEP left
Body length - 4 ft 8 in (1.4 m)
Femur length - 7 in (18 cm)

ROE DEER right
Body length - 3 ft (1 m)
Femur length - 7 in (18 cm)

The smallest bones in the body

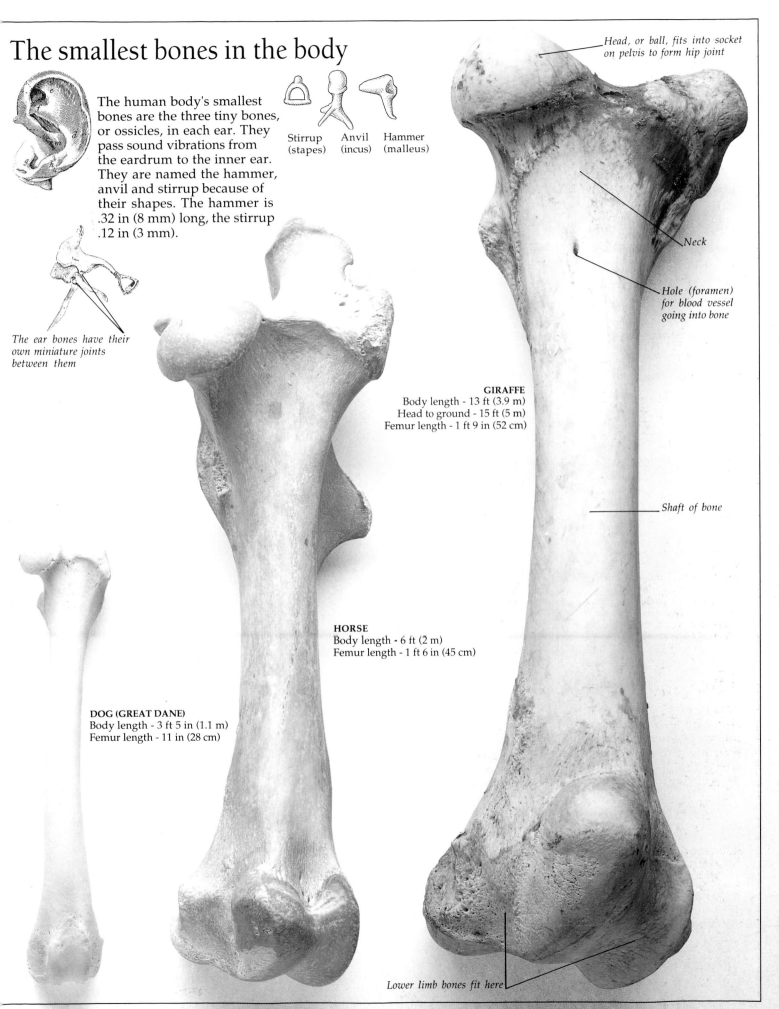

The human body's smallest bones are the three tiny bones, or ossicles, in each ear. They pass sound vibrations from the eardrum to the inner ear. They are named the hammer, anvil and stirrup because of their shapes. The hammer is .32 in (8 mm) long, the stirrup .12 in (3 mm).

Stirrup (stapes)

Anvil (incus)

Hammer (malleus)

The ear bones have their own miniature joints between them

Head, or ball, fits into socket on pelvis to form hip joint

Neck

Hole (foramen) for blood vessel going into bone

GIRAFFE
Body length - 13 ft (3.9 m)
Head to ground - 15 ft (5 m)
Femur length - 1 ft 9 in (52 cm)

Shaft of bone

HORSE
Body length - 6 ft (2 m)
Femur length - 1 ft 6 in (45 cm)

DOG (GREAT DANE)
Body length - 3 ft 5 in (1.1 m)
Femur length - 11 in (28 cm)

Lower limb bones fit here

Structure and repair of bones

LIVING BONES ARE NOT PALE, dry, and brittle, as they are in a museum case. Bone in the body is a busy living tissue. It is one-third water; it has blood vessels going in and out of it, supplying oxygen and nutrients and taking away wastes; certain bones contain marrow which produces blood cells; and bones have nerves that can feel pressure and pain. Bone is also a mineral store, containing calcium and other chemicals which give it hardness and rigidity. However, bone will give up its minerals in times of shortage, when other parts of the body (such as nerves) need them more. Bone tissue is made and maintained by several types of cells. Osteoblasts make new bone by hardening the protein collagen with minerals. Osteocytes maintain bone, passing nutrients and wastes back and forth between the blood and bone tissues. Osteoclasts destroy bone, releasing the minerals into the blood. All through life, bone is continually being reconstructed and reshaped as a result of the stresses, bends, and breaks it endures.

ISOTOPE SCAN
Radioactive isotopes concentrate in bone, and a scan shows their distribution in the skeleton.

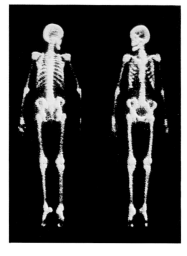

LIVING BONE
There are many ways of looking at living bones besides x-rays. By means of a pulsing crystal, this "scintigram" detects the concentrations of a radioactive isotope, which is injected into the body and taken up by bone tissue.

Inside bone

Bones are living examples of the engineer's art of design. Most bones have an outer "shell" of hard, solid, ivory-like compact bone. Tendons, ligaments, and other parts attach to this rigid shell by way of the living bone's "skin," the periosteum. Inside the compact bone is a looser, lighter network of spongy bone that contains the marrow.

Spongy bone

CURVED REINFORCEMENT
The Eiffel Tower's curved girders increase strength. The inside of the thigh bone is similarly reinforced.

Compact bone

TUBULAR DESIGN *left*
The compact bone forms a solid tube around the spongy bone. This thigh bone has had part of the compact bone cut away.

Spongy bone

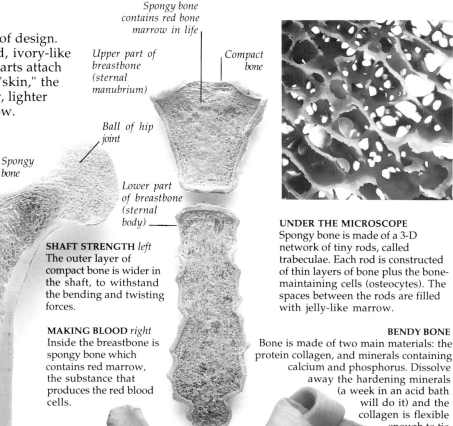

Spongy bone contains red bone marrow in life

Upper part of breastbone (sternal manubrium)

Compact bone

Ball of hip joint

Lower part of breastbone (sternal body)

SHAFT STRENGTH *left*
The outer layer of compact bone is wider in the shaft, to withstand the bending and twisting forces.

MAKING BLOOD *right*
Inside the breastbone is spongy bone which contains red marrow, the substance that produces the red blood cells.

Wide layer of compact bone for strength

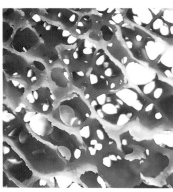

UNDER THE MICROSCOPE
Spongy bone is made of a 3-D network of tiny rods, called trabeculae. Each rod is constructed of thin layers of bone plus the bone-maintaining cells (osteocytes). The spaces between the rods are filled with jelly-like marrow.

BENDY BONE
Bone is made of two main materials: the protein collagen, and minerals containing calcium and phosphorus. Dissolve away the hardening minerals (a week in an acid bath will do it) and the collagen is flexible enough to tie in a knot!

Breaks and mends

Since bone is an active living tissue, it can usually mend itself after a crack or break (fracture). The gap is bridged first by fiber-like material, to form a scar or callus. Then bone-making cells (osteoblasts) gradually move into the callus and harden it into true bone. This is usually a little lumpy around the edges, so bone-destroying cells (osteoclasts) sculpt the bumps to produce a smooth mend.

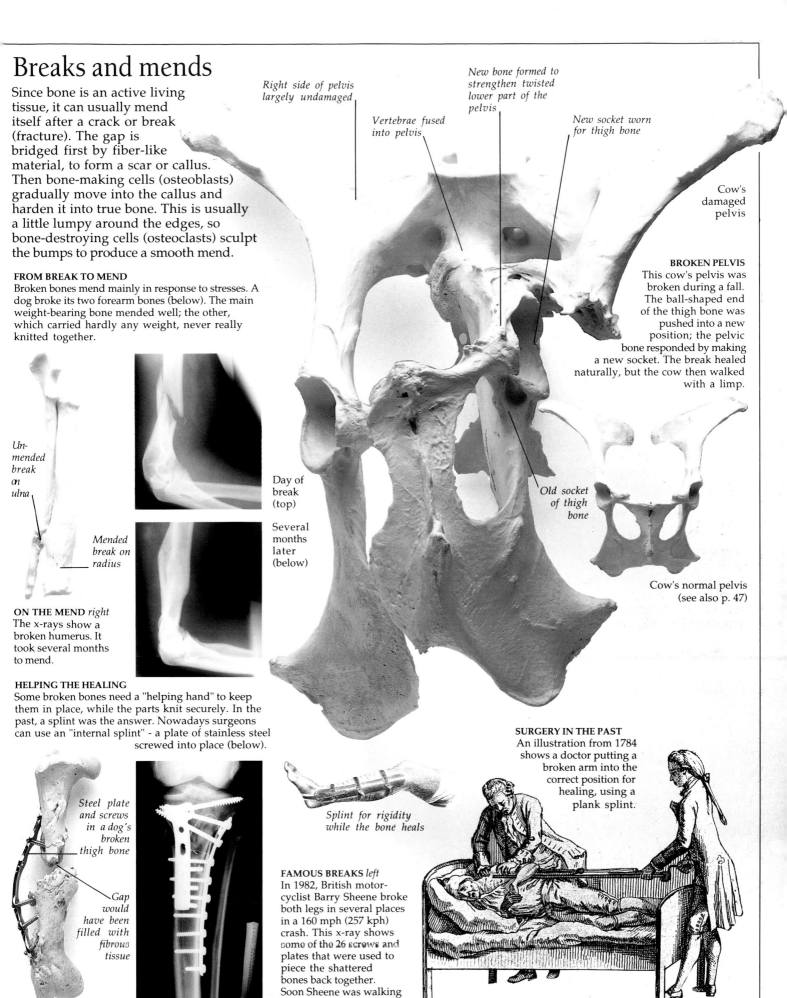

FROM BREAK TO MEND
Broken bones mend mainly in response to stresses. A dog broke its two forearm bones (below). The main weight-bearing bone mended well; the other, which carried hardly any weight, never really knitted together.

Un-mended break on ulna

Mended break on radius

ON THE MEND *right*
The x-rays show a broken humerus. It took several months to mend.

HELPING THE HEALING
Some broken bones need a "helping hand" to keep them in place, while the parts knit securely. In the past, a splint was the answer. Nowadays surgeons can use an "internal splint" - a plate of stainless steel screwed into place (below).

Steel plate and screws in a dog's broken thigh bone

Gap would have been filled with fibrous tissue

Right side of pelvis largely undamaged

Vertebrae fused into pelvis

New bone formed to strengthen twisted lower part of the pelvis

New socket worn for thigh bone

Cow's damaged pelvis

BROKEN PELVIS
This cow's pelvis was broken during a fall. The ball-shaped end of the thigh bone was pushed into a new position; the pelvic bone responded by making a new socket. The break healed naturally, but the cow then walked with a limp.

Day of break (top)

Several months later (below)

Old socket of thigh bone

Cow's normal pelvis (see also p. 47)

SURGERY IN THE PAST
An illustration from 1784 shows a doctor putting a broken arm into the correct position for healing, using a plank splint.

Splint for rigidity while the bone heals

FAMOUS BREAKS *left*
In 1982, British motor-cyclist Barry Sheene broke both legs in several places in a 160 mph (257 kph) crash. This x-ray shows some of the 26 screws and plates that were used to piece the shattered bones back together. Soon Sheene was walking - and riding - again.

Glossary of bone names

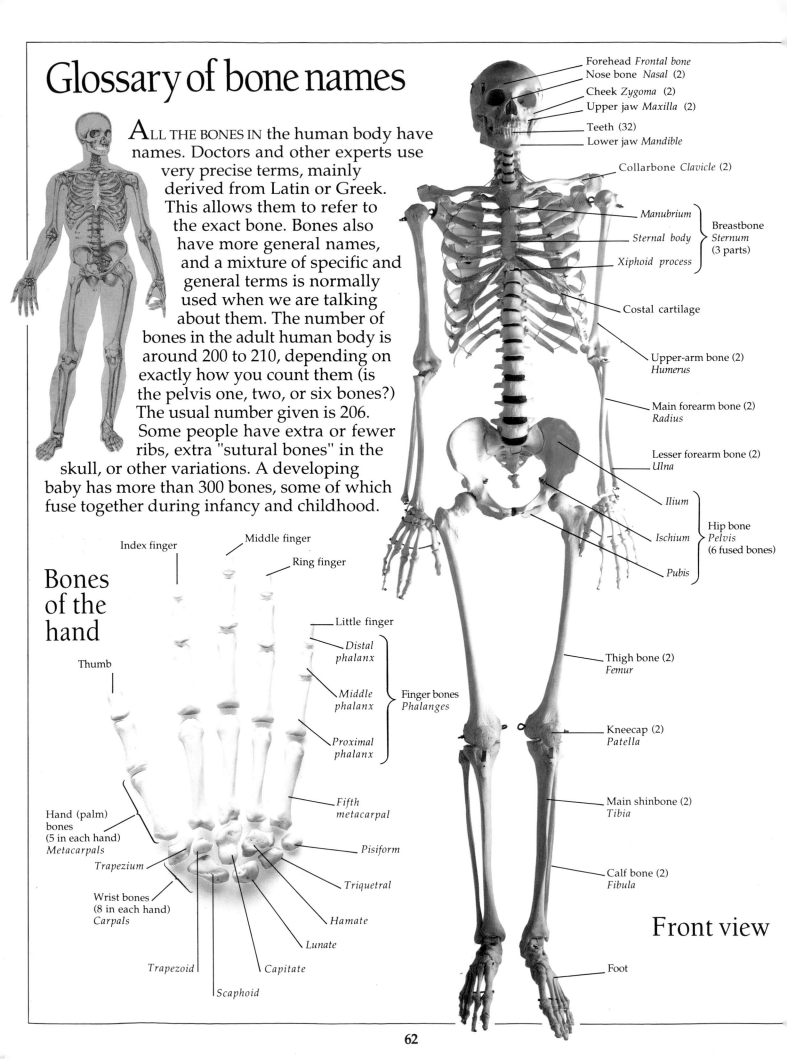

ALL THE BONES IN the human body have names. Doctors and other experts use very precise terms, mainly derived from Latin or Greek. This allows them to refer to the exact bone. Bones also have more general names, and a mixture of specific and general terms is normally used when we are talking about them. The number of bones in the adult human body is around 200 to 210, depending on exactly how you count them (is the pelvis one, two, or six bones?) The usual number given is 206. Some people have extra or fewer ribs, extra "sutural bones" in the skull, or other variations. A developing baby has more than 300 bones, some of which fuse together during infancy and childhood.

Forehead *Frontal bone*
Nose bone *Nasal* (2)
Cheek *Zygoma* (2)
Upper jaw *Maxilla* (2)
Teeth (32)
Lower jaw *Mandible*

Collarbone *Clavicle* (2)

Manubrium
Sternal body
Xiphoid process
Breastbone *Sternum* (3 parts)

Costal cartilage

Upper-arm bone (2) *Humerus*

Main forearm bone (2) *Radius*

Lesser forearm bone (2) *Ulna*

Ilium
Ischium
Pubis
Hip bone *Pelvis* (6 fused bones)

Thigh bone (2) *Femur*

Kneecap (2) *Patella*

Main shinbone (2) *Tibia*

Calf bone (2) *Fibula*

Foot

Front view

Bones of the hand

Index finger
Middle finger
Ring finger
Little finger

Thumb

Distal phalanx
Middle phalanx
Proximal phalanx
Finger bones *Phalanges*

Fifth metacarpal

Hand (palm) bones (5 in each hand) *Metacarpals*

Trapezium

Wrist bones (8 in each hand) *Carpals*

Pisiform
Triquetral
Hamate
Lunate
Capitate
Scaphoid
Trapezoid

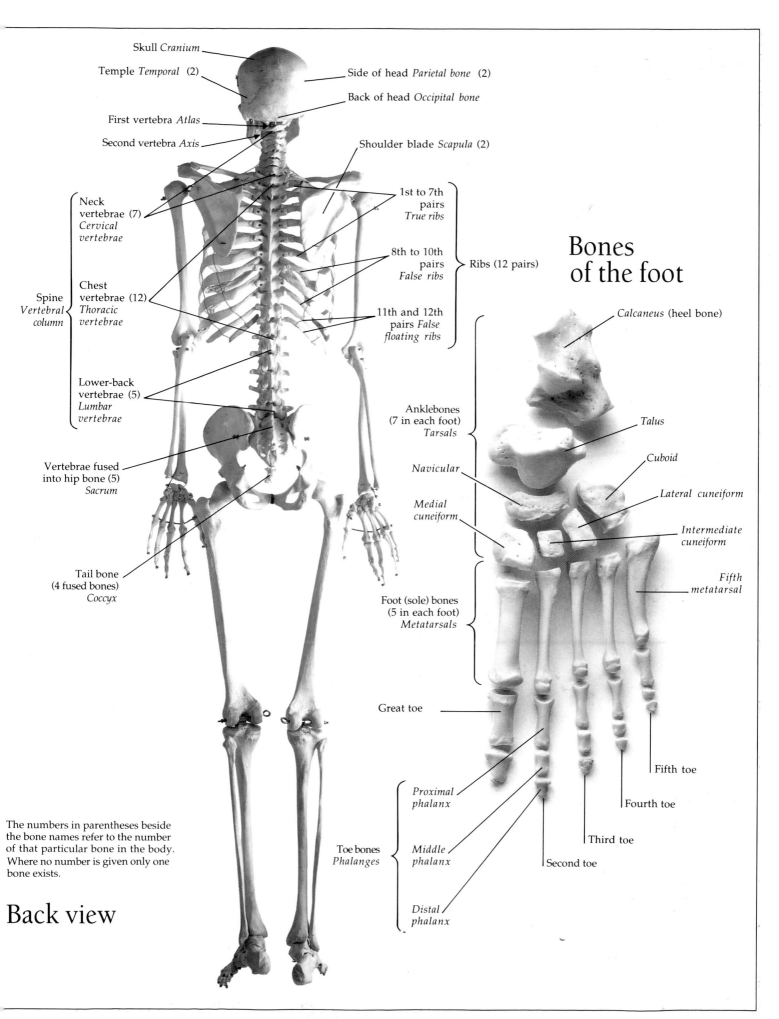

Skull *Cranium*

Temple *Temporal* (2)

Side of head *Parietal bone* (2)

Back of head *Occipital bone*

First vertebra *Atlas*

Second vertebra *Axis*

Shoulder blade *Scapula* (2)

Neck
vertebrae (7)
*Cervical
vertebrae*

1st to 7th
pairs
True ribs

Ribs (12 pairs)

Bones
of the foot

Spine
*Vertebral
column*

Chest
vertebrae (12)
*Thoracic
vertebrae*

8th to 10th
pairs
False ribs

Calcaneus (heel bone)

11th and 12th
pairs *False
floating ribs*

Anklebones
(7 in each foot)
Tarsals

Talus

Cuboid

Navicular

Lateral cuneiform

Lower-back
vertebra (5)
*Lumbar
vertebrae*

*Medial
cuneiform*

*Intermediate
cuneiform*

Vertebrae fused
into hip bone (5)
Sacrum

*Fifth
metatarsal*

Foot (sole) bones
(5 in each foot)
Metatarsals

Tail bone
(4 fused bones)
Coccyx

Great toe

Fifth toe

Fourth toe

Third toe

The numbers in parentheses beside
the bone names refer to the number
of that particular bone in the body.
Where no number is given only one
bone exists.

Toe bones
Phalanges

*Proximal
phalanx*

*Middle
phalanx*

Second toe

*Distal
phalanx*

Back view

Index

Acknowledgments

Dorling Kindersley would like to thank:
The Booth Museum of Natural History, Brighton, Peter Gardiner, Griffin and George, The Royal College of Surgeons of England, The Royal Veterinary College, and Paul Vos for skeletal material.
Dr A.V. Mitchell for the X-rays.
Richard and Hilary Bird for the index.
Fred Ford and Mike Pilley of Radius Graphics, and Ray Owen and Nick Madren for artwork.
Anne-Marie Bulat for her work on the initial stages of the book.
Dave King for special photography on pages 14-20 and pages 32-3.

Picture credits

t=top b=bottom m=middle l=left r=right

Des and Jen Bartlett/Bruce Coleman Ltd: 51tl
Des and Jen Bartlett/Survival Anglia: 57b
Erwin and Peggy Bauer/Bruce Coleman Ltd: 47t
BPCC/Aldus Archive: 9b; 10t, mr, br; 11t; 29b
Bridgeman Art Library: 8m; 9ml; 10ml; 11ml
Jane Burton/Bruce Coleman Ltd: 33m
A. Campbell/NHPA: 34b
CNRI/Science Photo Library: 26m; 49tr; 55br; 60tl
Bruce Coleman Ltd: 51br
A. Davies/NHPA: 34t
Elsdint/Science Photo Library: 60 tl
Francisco Eriza/Bruce Coleman Ltd: 50b
Jeff Foott/Survival Anglia: 50mr 42m; 48m; 54m
John Freeman, London: 6bl; 7t; Tom and Pam Gardener/Frank Lane Picture Agency: 33t
P. Goycolea/Alan Hutchison Library: 11bl

Sonia Halliday Photographs: 43b
E. Hanumantha Rao/NHPA: 53b
Julian Hector/Planet Earth Pictures: 50t
T.Henshaw/Daily Telegraph Colour Library: 54br
Michael Holford: 9t; 11mr; 36t
Eric Hosking: 33br; 51bl; 52tr; 56m
F Jack Jackson/Planet Earth Pictures: 41
Antony Joyce/Planet Earth Pictures: 33br
Gordon Langsbury/Bruce Coleman Ltd: 32tr
Michael Leach/NHPA: 56t
Lacz Lemoine/NHPA: 32mr
Mansell Collection: 6m; 7m; 15t; 36m; 43t; 56mr; 58t; 61br
Marineland/Frank Lane Picture Agency: 51m
Mary Evans Picture Library: 6tl, br; 7b; 8t, b; 9mr; 10bl; 11br; 13br; 14l, r; 16ml; 26t; 45br; 58ml, mr; 62tl
Frieder Michler/Science Photo Library: 60m
Geoff Moon/Frank Lane Picture Agency: 32br
Alfred Pasieka/Bruce Coleman Ltd: 22t
Philip Perry/Frank Lane Picture

Agency: 35t
Dieter and Mary Plage/Bruce Coleman Ltd: 40b
Hans Reinhard/Bruce Coleman Ltd: 32bl; 46bl
Leonard Lee Rue/Bruce Coleman Ltd: 32ml; 52ml
Keith Scholey/Planet Earth Pictures: 50ml
Johnathan Scott/Planet Earth Pictures: 37bl
Silvestris/Frank Lane Picture Agency:35b
Syndication International: 61bl
Terry Whittaker/Frank Lane Picture Agency: 52bl
ZEFA: 37t; 39tr; 60b
Gunter Ziesler/Bruce Coleman Ltd: 37br

Illustrations by Will Giles: 12b; 13t, m; 27l, r; 28b; 29t; 34bl, m; 35tl, br; 37m; 38b; 39l; 42b; 44bl, bm, br; 45bl, bm; 46ml, mr, b; 47ml, mr, bl, br; 48ml; 49m; 51tr; 52m, b; 53t, ml, mr; 54bm; 55m; 56t; 59tm

Picture research by: Millie Trowbridge